COUNTRY MUSIC U.S.A.

FROM NASHVILLE TO BRANSON

MICHAEL McCALL

PUBLICATIONS INTERNATIONAL, LTD.

Michael McCall is a Nashville based country music and entertainment writer whose credits include a biography of Garth Brooks and articles in *US* and *Billboard.* He served as music critic and feature writer for the *Nashville Banner* for seven years and currently reports on the country music scene for the *Los Angeles Times* and *Pulse Magazine.*

Contributing Writers:
Dave Hoakstra is the country music writer for the *Chicago Sun-Times,* where his features and columns on country music, entertainment, and popular culture have appeared since 1981. As contributing editor to *Chicago Magazine,* he provided critical commentary and stories on rock, jazz, and blues music and Chicago nightlife.

Janet Williams, a Nashville resident, has closely followed the country music scene by interviewing performers and writing features in her role as associate editor of *Close Up,* the magazine of the Country Music Association. Previously, she served as an associate producer of USA Network's *Night Flight.*

Photo credits
Front cover: (clockwise, from upper left corner): **E.J. Camp/Outline Press; David Redfern/Retna USA; Barry Wolfe/Globe Photos, Inc.; Wayne Williams/Outline Press; Lynn McAfee/Shooting Star; Mark Weiss/MWA; Globe Photos, Inc.:** Lynn McAfee; Beth Gwinn; Lloyd Dinkin; Lynn McAfee; **John Paschal/Celebrity Photo. Back cover: Baldknobbers Music Theater** (bottom); **FPG International:** Dave Davis (center); Travelpix (top).

Arista Records: 46; **Baldknobbers Music Theater:** 80 (top); **Matt Bradley:** 75; **Anita Bugge/Fotex:** 68; **Bambe Levine Picture, Inc.:** 79; **Buck Trent Music Theater:** 78; **Celebrity Photo:** Tammie Arroyo: 19 (bottom), 25; Greg DeGuire: 43 (right); John Paschal: 31, 34; **Cristy Lane Theater:** 73; **FPG International:** James Blank: 63; Riley Caton: 44; Kent Knudson: 61; Buddy Mays: 60; **Gamma Liaison:** John Barr: 42; Alain Benainous: 3 (bottom right); Borsari: 70; Paul S. Howell: 27; Steve Lowry/Nashville Banner: 29 (bottom), 35; Elizabeth Marshall: 22; George Rose: 30; Renato Rotolo: 76; James Schnepf: 10; Bob Scott: 29 (top); **Mark E. Gibson:** 5, 45; **Globe Photos, Inc.:** Lynn McAfee: 71, 77; Adam Scull: 69 (top); **International Stock Photography:** Kit Luce: 4; Randy Masser: 7 (right center); G.E. Pakenham: 7 (top); Beatriz Schiller: 7 (left center); **London Features International USA:** Simon Fowler: 6; Phil Loftus: 65; Ron Wolfson: 48, 54, 64, 67 (right); **Alan L. Mayor:** 19 (top), 23, 33, 59 (top); **R.L. McCowan:** 62; **McGuire/MCA Records:** 24; **Michael Murphy/Texas Department of Commerce**: 59 (bottom); **Onyx:** Edie Baskin: 11; Chris Carroll: 41; Henry Diltz: 11; Blake Little: 12; Firooz Zahedi: 28; **Outline Press:** Michael Baytoff: 3 (left); C. Blankenhorn: 57; E.J. Camp: 36, 38; Geoffrey Croft: 53 (left); Lee Crum: 32; Bob Greene: 74; Lauren Hicks: 51, 58; George Lange: 37 (bottom), 47; Frank Micelotta: 14, 43 (left); Paul Natkin: 50; Mike Norcia: 49 (bottom); Neal Preston: 13, 66; Ken Sax/Naras: 39, 52; Robin Thomas: 49 (top); **Will Van Overbeek/©1991 Warner Bros. Records/Reprise Records:** 56; **Presley's Theater:** 80 (bottom); **RCA Records:** 26; **Retna USA:** Jay Blakesberg: 53 (right); Larry Busacca: 9; Steve Granitz: 15; Beth Gwinn: 17, 20, 55; Lynn McAfee: 72; Susan Rutman: 16; **Shooting Star:** Erik Heinila: 69 (bottom); Yoram Kahana: 67 (left); Lynn McAfee: 8; Ron Mesaros: 3 (top right); Marc Morrison: 18; Michael Virden: 40; Rudy Willis: 37 (top); **Superstock:** 7 (bottom); **Mark Weiss/MWA:** 21.

Contents

Nashville Music City, U.S.A.

Nashville has been the home of the Grand Ole Opry since its 1925 start. The Opry moved to its new suburban-based Opry House in 1974 (this page). Nashville (opposite) became known as Music City, U.S.A., in the 1950s.

Guitarist Chet Atkins is frequently asked to describe the music of Nashville. More often than not, the famous musician and record producer will stick his hand in a pants pocket and jiggle some coins. "That," he jokes, "is the Nashville Sound."

With this bit of wry humor, Atkins suggests that in Nashville, the sound of country music is shaped as much by commerce as by artistic impulse. It is the well-honed ability to turn country music into a commercial sound that has transformed Nashville into the country music capital. In regions such as the Southwest, music communities are known for encouraging individual expression; in Nashville, the music community is known—and sometimes criticized—for molding performers to fit popular formulas easily accepted by radio stations and record buyers. "Nashville is more than a music town," Atkins says. "It is a music-business town."

Nashville is the American city most closely identified with the music made within its borders. Nashville's nickname, "Music City, U.S.A.," first rolled off the lips of local disc jockey David Cobb in 1950. The catchy phrase has since proved to be a brilliant marketing term for promoting the city's best-known industry. However, at the time Cobb gave Nashville its slogan, it was more fanciful boast than supportable fact. In 1950, only three number-one songs had been recorded in Nashville.

At mid-century, people no more identified country music with Nashville than they did with Chicago, Atlanta, Cincinnati, or Fort Worth—all cities where important country music recordings were made during World War II. However, after

WKDA

the war, Nashville began assembling the machinery that could roll out the hits smoothly and efficiently.

Most important was the emergence of the Grand Ole Opry as the biggest of the many live radio shows that beamed country music into homes throughout America. The Opry had Roy Acuff, the nation's best-known country star in the 1940s; it also had Ernest Tubb, Eddy Arnold, Hank Williams, Flatt & Scruggs, and Hank Snow.

The Opry stayed strong, even against new, unforeseen forces in entertainment. Television began luring listeners away from radio, and many stations responded by decreasing the time devoted to live barn dances and jamborees. But WSM Radio continued to air the Grand Ole Opry. The station's owner, National Life and Accident Insurance, considered the 50,000-watt, clear-channel Opry broadcast a great promotional tool for selling policies to rural families throughout the South and Midwest.

As the program's influence grew, an invitation to join the Opry's performance roster became an important career step for any ambitious country music singer set on national stardom. With talent flocking to Nashville, several savvy performers and radio executives decided to branch out into recording, song publishing, and concert booking. In doing so, they pioneered what has

Roy Acuff, known as the King of Country Music, was the Grand Ole Opry's first superstar. He performed on the show from 1938 until shortly before his death.

become a multimillion dollar music industry for Nashville.

The pioneers included Opry patriarch Roy Acuff, who loaned WSM executive Fred Rose the money to start a publishing company. Acuff-Rose became the first successful company to concentrate solely on publishing country music songs. Two other cornerstone country music publishing companies, Cedarwood and Tree, were also started by former WSM employees. As songwriting took a bigger role in the financial structure of the music business, these companies flourished.

Three former Opry engineers opened Nashville's first professional music studio. Opry stars quickly found that scheduling time at Castle Recording Company was infinitely more convenient than traveling to New York or Chicago. When Acuff, Tubb, Williams, and Red Foley shifted their recording work to Castle, Nashville was on its way to becoming a recording capital.

Decca Records noticed the action coming out of Nashville and hired pianist and band conductor Owen Bradley to open an office in town. Bradley went on to record Decca classics by Tubb, Foley, Loretta Lynn, Conway Twitty, and others. RCA soon followed suit, hiring a young guitarist named Chet Atkins to serve as a recording director. Atkins immediately went to work creating smoothly produced hits by Arnold, Snow, Jim Reeves, Don Gibson, Elvis Presley, and others. These producers helped keep country music afloat in the early rock 'n' roll era.

As Nashville's reputation as a music center grew, it began attracting devoted fans who wanted to do more than hear the music; they yearned to see it, to photograph it. The Grand Ole Opry has drawn more than 12,000 fans per weekend for four decades because it provides an opportunity to hear and see such icons as Chet Atkins and Bill Monroe, as well as such new superstars as Garth Brooks and Randy Travis.

The Opry now presents its homegrown music inside the modern 4,400-seat Opry House, located within the confines of the Opryland entertainment complex. Nonetheless, visitors still line up to walk through the Opry's most famous home, the Ryman Auditorium, a rustic former tabernacle in downtown Nashville. Known as "the Mother Church of Country

Music," the Ryman provided intimate accommodations for the Opry from 1943 to 1974.

Around the corner from the Ryman is Tootsie's Orchid Lounge. Tootsie's was once the favored watering hole for Opry performers, who zipped out the Ryman's back door and into the bar through a special alley entrance. Across Broadway from Tootsie's sits the Ernest Tubb Record Shop, which opened around the corner in 1947 before settling into its current location a few years later. *The Ernest Tubb Midnight Jamboree* was broadcast every Saturday night for decades from the store's showroom before moving to a second ET record store near Opryland.

Nashville flaunts plenty of other sights for the music-minded tourist. The celebrated Music Row area combines sedate business offices with glitzy tourist attractions. The heart and soul of the city's music attractions can be found at the Country Music Hall of Fame and Museum. Down the road, neon signs compete for attention by flashing the names and images of country music favorites. There's the Country Music Wax Museum, as well as various-sized gift shops bearing the names of Barbara Mandrell, Loretta Lynn, George Strait, Randy Travis, and others. There are many other attractions all over the city too numerous to mention.

Nashville has forged a lucrative industry out of pleasing its fans.

The Ryman Auditorium (top) was home to the Grand Ole Opry from 1943 to 1974. When the Opry moved to Opryland, it became part of a theme park that includes rides for the kids (middle, left). The Ernest Tubb Record Store No. 1 (middle, right), a downtown institution for decades, is one of many businesses sporting the names of country stars. The Country Music Hall of Fame and Museum (bottom) is a renowned repository of historical research and memorabilia.

Alabama

While playing in South Carolina in the mid-1970s, Alabama covered songs by musicians as diverse as Van Morrison and George Jones.

Perhaps it's the nonconformist outlaw image, but throughout the history of country music, rugged solo artists have overshadowed most duets and groups. Until Alabama came along.

The band has been honored many times by the Country Music Association, winning the prestigious Entertainer of the Year award in 1982, 1983, and 1984. In addition, Alabama has won two Grammys and, from 1980 to 1987, they notched many number-one country records.

Alabama came together in Fort Payne, Alabama, a town of about 12,000 people at the foot of the Lookout Mountains. Lead singer Randy Owen, keyboardist and lead guitarist Jeff Cook, and bass guitarist Teddy Gentry are cousins, but they didn't start playing together until 1970. Their first band was Wild Country. Another cousin, Jackie Owen, was the group's first drummer. In 1973 he was replaced by Mark Herndon, a nonrelative. Alabama's earliest shows were at the Canyonland amusement park outside of Fort Payne.

In 1973, Alabama moved to Myrtle Beach, South Carolina. Thanks in part to the rapid turnover of the resort crowds, the band was able to perform an eclectic repertoire, including covers of rock hits as well as rocking versions of country hits.

By 1980, the group was playing more original material and had established its trademark polished harmonies. Randy Owens's lead vocals, reminiscent of Glenn Frey of the Eagles, caught the ear of several record companies. In 1981, Alabama signed with RCA Records. The group went on to sell 45 million records during the 1980s. By the 1990s, the group sounded more like a pop-rock band than a country band.

No longer as novel as they once were, Alabama has seen some of its rock-oriented appeal diminished by the advent of such acts as Garth Brooks and Clint Black, who use rock 'n' roll-style lighting, staging, and songs to cross over from country in search of a wider audience.

Clint Black

When Clint Black called his third album *The Hard Way*, he might have been referring to his difficulties in severing relations with a business manager and in fighting with his record company for more creative control. But not all his recent life has been hard. Black says two events will heavily influence his future. He married actress Lisa Hartman, and he performed and recorded with one of his idols, Roy Rogers.

Black was born in New Jersey but raised in Texas. By the time he was 15, he was playing guitar, bass, and harmonica. Starting in 1981, he lived a hand-to-mouth existence for six years on the Houston club circuit. During one engagement, he met songwriter Hayden Nicholas. After the two began writing songs together, Black took steps to get a record deal. He used Nicholas's eight-track home recording studio to make a demo tape.

The finished tape found its way to Bill Ham, manager of rock band ZZ Top. Ham was struck by the lyrics and Black's distinctive vocals. After hooking up with Ham, Black met Joe Galante, then head of RCA Records Nashville division. Clint strolled into his office and played four demos. Galante agreed to fly to Houston to see him perform, and Black soon signed an eight album contract.

Black's debut album, *Killin' Time*, earned Clint a number of awards, including the Country Music Association's Horizon Award, American Music Award for New Artist of the Year, and four Academy of Country Music Awards. Black's second album, *Put Yourself in My Shoes*, was received just as enthusiastically as its predecessor.

Black seemed dedicated to his career—until he met actress Lisa Hartman following a New Year's Eve performance in 1990. A romance blossomed, and they were married on October 20, 1991.

Black's latest album, *The Hard Way*, was released in the summer of 1992.

The video of Black's first single, "A Better Man," was released in May 1989, making Black an instant hit. It went to number one on the country charts.

Garth Brooks

Brooks writes about half the songs on his albums; rodeo cowboys are a recurring subject.

Garth Brooks has set a new standard for country music success. In an unprecedented feat for a country artist, Garth's third album, *Ropin' the Wind*, reached the number-one spot on *Billboard*'s pop music charts the first week of its release. While both Johnny Cash and Kenny Rogers have reached the top of the pop charts, they did so only after weeks of sales.

To the pop music industry, this brash country singer seemed to emerge from nowhere. While Brooks insists that he's just a fun-loving, regular guy playing the music he loves, others maintain he possesses the inner strength to follow his convictions. He's tackled subjects outside the conventions of Nashville and invested a wild-eyed energy into his performances.

A native Oklahoman, Garth Brooks was the sixth and last child to join the clan of Troyal and Colleen Brooks. Brooks didn't pick up a guitar until he was a junior in high school. After graduation, he attended Oklahoma State University on an athletic scholarship. While in college, Brooks started performing in nightclubs. At first he performed solo; before long, however, he joined a band.

After finishing college in 1985, Brooks set out for Nashville and a country music career. He lasted 23 hours! A meeting with a music executive left him so discouraged he returned to Oklahoma to assess his future.

Two years later, Brooks returned to Nashville accompanied by his bride of one year, Sandy Mahl. This time, Brooks had better luck. Just eight months after he arrived in Nashville, Brooks signed a recording contract with Capitol Records. When Capitol introduced him to record producer Allen Reynolds, Brooks's approach to music began to take shape. Reynolds, who produced Brooks's first album, *Garth Brooks*, suggested that Brooks stop singing ballads in a full-voiced, operatic style. The producer encouraged Brooks to relax and sing in a gentler, more natural manner. Reynolds's coaching later proved key to Brooks's success in conveying the tender emotion of the ballads "If Tomorrow Never Comes" and "The Dance."

Brooks's second album, *No Fences*, sold 700,000 copies the first ten days it was in stores. The first week of October 1990, as his first and second albums both crossed the million mark in sales, Brooks became a member of the Grand Ole Opry. Sales of his first three albums have now crossed the 20 million mark. Brooks's latest records include a Christmas album, *Beyond the Season*, and *The Chase*.

Brooks has won plenty of awards from the Academy of Country Music and the Country Music Association, including the prestigious Entertainer of the Year honors at both pageants in 1991. He also won American Music awards for Best Male Country Artist, Best Country Single for "The Thunder Rolls," and Best Country Album for *No Fences*.

In concert, Garth Brooks's onstage enthusiasm sends the crowd into hysterics. He'll do almost anything for a response: sprint across the stage, dangle from a ladder, or douse himself with water. Mainstream American audiences were introduced to his maniacal performing style when the dynamic singer was featured in a TV special titled *This Is Garth Brooks* in January 1992.

Above: Garth Brooks promises to keep coming up with surprises for his concerts. *Below:* While on tour, Brooks employs family members in his band as well as behind the scenes.

Mary-Chapin Carpenter

Mary-Chapin Carpenter—who blends several different musical styles—has a warm alto voice that draws fans from diverse backgrounds.

Mary-Chapin Carpenter stood on stage looking out at several thousand members of the Country Music Association. She had just been named its 1992 Female Vocalist of the Year. "I didn't expect this at all," she said. The trophy completed Carpenter's unlikely climb to the top ranks of country music stardom. Her literate songwriting and sassy, intimate vocal style, along with good timing and a strange twist of fate helped her reach that height.

In 1987, Mary-Chapin Carpenter recorded some songs in the basement studio of her longtime guitarist, John Jennings. She wanted to make a tape of her music to sell in the Washington, D.C., clubs she had been playing. The tape reached a CBS Records executive, who offered her a record deal. With one new song added, the tape became Carpenter's debut album, *Hometown Girl.*

She was hardly a conventional country music prospect. Born in Princeton, New Jersey, and raised in Tokyo and Washington, D.C., Carpenter grew up in an upper-middle-class, urban household. She attended Brown University. Her musical tastes leaned toward rock 'n' roll and folk singers.

In high school, she spent many hours strumming her guitar in her bedroom. Her first performance was at an open-mike night at a local club. She continued to perform through college, pursuing a musical career more vigorously after graduation.

Her commercial breakthrough came with *State of the Heart,* her second album for Columbia Records. The album earned her an Academy of Country Music award for Top New Female Artist. Her success continued with her third disc, *Shooting Straight in the Dark.* In this album, Carpenter continued to probe a wide emotional range with personal insight and keenly observed detail, revealing the folk influence on her music. Her latest album, *Come On Come On,* was released in the summer of 1992 and was certified gold within weeks.

Carlene Carter

Carlene Carter spent more than a decade recording country-flavored rock in such outposts as London, Los Angeles, and New York before finally coming home to Nashville in 1990.

Carlene Carter's family tree has the deepest roots in country music. Granddaughter of Maybelle Carter, Carlene's parents are June Carter Cash and Carl Smith. Johnny Cash is her stepfather, and Goldie Hill, a popular country singer during the 1950's, is her stepmother. Carter's extended family includes stepsister Rosanne Cash and former brothers-in-law Marty Stuart and Rodney Crowell.

Carter found herself with a hit country album in 1990 when Warner Bros. Records released *I Fell in Love.* But before finding success as a country performer, Carter ventured into other types of music. She began defining her musical style while attending Nashville's Belmont College and landed her first record deal in 1978. Her quest for her own sound led from her country roots to pop to rhythm and blues and then to England. There she was married for a short time to rock singer Nick Lowe.

With five albums under her belt but no hits to her credit, Carter sought success as a songwriter. Such diverse acts as Emmylou Harris and the Doobie Brothers recorded her songs. Carlene credits her mother, June Carter Cash, for the motivation to start writing.

In 1990, Carter became Nashville's unofficial homecoming queen when she not only returned to her country roots but also moved back to Music City. Three years earlier, she had joined the Carter Family for a London performance and toured with the group for two years. Her varied experiences and explorations of different musical styles definitely influenced the *I Fell in Love* album. Combining the bluegrass-inspired gospel of the Carter Family with the rockabilly sound of Nick Lowe, Carter has forged a mature style that is uniquely her own.

Carlene Carter's *I Fell in Love* climbed to number three on *Billboard*'s country chart. The title track garnered much recognition and praise.

Rosanne Cash avoids a formulaic approach to songwriting; many of her deeply personal songs explore the ambiguities of modern relationships.

Rosanne Cash was standing on stage introducing a shatteringly personal song when she admitted, "I used to not feel comfortable singing this one, but then I saw Lou Reed and I realized you can say anything you want to. Eight years of therapy, one night of Lou Reed. . . ."

As the statement suggests, Rosanne Cash may belong to one of country music's most famous families, but she is no common country music personality. She recorded her first album in Germany, her second in Los Angeles. She was critical of the old Nashville recording system and has never paid attention to the formulas adhered to by most country hit-makers. She was the only woman to have a number-one country album through the early and mid-1980s, and she has topped the country charts 12 times.

Cash was born in Memphis in 1955. At 11, she moved with her father, Johnny Cash, and mother, Vivian Liberto, to California. Her father divorced Vivian shortly afterward. Rosanne remained with her mother but maintained a close relationship with her father. After high school, she joined her father's road show. She eventually left the band to live in England for a year and then returned to study drama.

In 1978, she met Rodney Crowell, a singer-songwriter who had just released his solo debut album. Crowell helped her produce some songs, which led to her traveling to Germany to record her first album for Arista records.

A CBS Records executive heard the album and signed her to a contract. With Crowell producing, she recorded *Right or Wrong*, released in 1979; she and Crowell married early that same year. The couple moved to Nashville and recorded *Seven Year Ache* in 1981.

Cash records and tours less frequently than most country performers, devoting time to motherhood, painting, and writing fiction. Her subsequent albums often explored her turbulent relationship with Crowell. The couple separated in 1991.

Billy Ray Cyrus

When Billy Ray Cyrus finished his first album for Mercury Records, the company's executives decided "Achy Breaky Heart" was a potential hit. But they feared the rock-influenced guitar work might meet resistance from radio. Mercury set up a promotion plan involving country dance clubs and country video stations. Long before the song reached radio, devoted dance club patrons loved the Achy Breaky Line Dance, and thousands of young women swooned as Cyrus performed on video. By the time radio received the song, the stations had already been flooded with requests. When Mercury released Cyrus's album, *Some Gave All*, it exploded onto the country and pop charts. It quickly moved to number one.

The sudden success of Billy Ray Cyrus proved that country music could create instantaneous stars as quickly as its pop and rock counterparts. For Cyrus, it fulfilled a lifelong obsession with becoming a nationally known music celebrity.

A native of Flatwoods, Kentucky, Cyrus spent two years in Los Angeles pursuing a music career before returning home in 1986 to form a band. He began performing at a club in nearby Huntington, West Virginia, blending original songs with covers of hits by Bob Seger, Lynyrd Skynyrd, and Led Zeppelin. On his days off, Cyrus drove to Nashville seeking an opportunity. Each stay lasted less than 24 hours, as he had to hustle back to Huntington for his next performance.

In 1989, his persistence paid off when he hooked up with manager Jack McFadden, who had worked with Buck Owens, Keith Whitley, and Lorrie Morgan. Two years later, Cyrus signed with Mercury Records. The singer won his first award from the Country Music Association in 1992 when "Achy Breaky Heart" was tabbed as Single of the Year. At this early stage in his career, Cyrus is as much a pop phenomenon as he is a country singer.

Billy Ray Cyrus's music shows a heavy rock 'n' roll influence. Whether Cyrus is just a flash in the pan remains to be seen.

Vince Gill

For most of the 1980s, many in country music predicted stardom for Vince Gill. But stardom always seemed just beyond his grasp. All that changed in the 1990s. By the fall of 1992, Gill had arrived at the top of country music. Within the same week, he co-hosted the Country Music Association Awards show and received awards for Male Vocalist of the Year and Song of the Year. His new album, *I Still Believe in You,* was ranked among the 10 best-selling albums. It all started in 1990 with "When I Call Your Name," his first song to go to the top of the charts.

An only child, Gill credits his father for piquing his interest in music. One of the first instruments young Gill played was his dad's banjo. Gill joined a local bluegrass band while still in high school.

Throughout the late 1970s, Gill paid his dues in a number of diverse bands, eventually hooking up with Rodney Crowell's band, the Cherry Bombs. Gill landed a solo deal through Tony Brown, a former member of the Cherry Bombs who worked for RCA Records. In 1984, Gill had a taste of success with his six-song mini-album, *Turn Me Loose.*

Gill enjoyed some further success on his second and third albums, but he failed to catch fire. Tony Brown, however, remained convinced of Gill's potential. Under a new label and new producer, Gill used the full range of his talent on *When I Call Your Name.*

In the fall of 1990, Gill gladly accepted the CMA Award for Single of the Year for "When I Call Your Name," starting a chain of awards and much-deserved recognition. Gill settled into a more clearly defined country style for his next album, *Pocket Full of Gold.* Gill became a member of the Grand Ole Opry in 1991.

Vince Gill is a man of many talents. Besides being one of the better guitar players in Nashville, Gill seriously considered a career in professional golf.

Alan Jackson

When Alan Jackson accepted the award for ASCAP Song of the Year for cowriting "Don't Rock the Jukebox," he could only shake his head. "I'm still stunned by everything," he said. His streak has continued with *A Lot About Livin' (And A Little 'Bout Love)*, his third album, released in the fall of 1992.

Jackson is one of the entertainers who helped country music become so popular in the early 1990s. He ranks among the top handsome male singers who appeal to a wide range of female fans. Some female fans were dismayed to learn Jackson is married. In fact, his wife, Denise, is largely responsible for his musical career.

In 1985, after a series of unsatisfying jobs, Jackson decided to try a career in music. He had no idea where to go or who to see. Denise saw Glen Campbell at the Atlanta airport and asked Campbell for his advice. He gave her the name of his publishing company in Nashville and told her to have Alan drop by. Armed with Campbell's business card, Jackson relocated to Nashville.

Through Campbell's organization, Jackson started playing honky tonks all across the country, honing his skills. In September 1989, Jackson signed with Arista Records. Jackson's debut album, *Here in the Real World*, soared to the number-four spot on *Billboard*'s country album chart. The Academy of Country Music named him Top New Male Artist in April 1991. Jackson's second album, *Don't Rock the Jukebox*, hit the jackpot.

Jackson, the youngest of five children, admits that singing country music was not something he seriously considered while growing up in Newnan, Georgia, but music was always a hobby. He met Denise when he was 17, and they married four years later. When in his 20s, Jackson had an undeniable urge to pursue a career in music. When Denise met Campbell, Jackson was on his way.

Alan Jackson had a big year in 1991. His second album, *Don't Rock the Jukebox*, went platinum, and he became a member of the Grand Ole Opry.

George Jones

Deep in the timber of a George Jones song, you can hear the soul of country music. The absolute purity of Jones's vocals assures that his style will influence Nashville music for generations to come.

A Country Music Association Male Vocalist of the Year spanning two decades (he won in 1962 and 1963 and in 1980 and 1981), Jones sings from the most cobwebbed corners of his heart. His textured voice reveals tension, with authoritative range running like a railroad train between honky-tonk and sorrow. Jones's trademark is his playful country flutter. He downcasts vocal lines for drama before immediately climbing the scale.

George—one of seven brothers—was born to Clara and George Washington Jones, Sr., on September 12, 1931, in Saratoga, Texas. "I never played guitar until church, although when I was very young, I sung around the house," Jones says. "My Sunday school teacher taught me my first chords on a guitar." Clara Jones was very religious and played organ and piano in church. George Washington Jones, Sr., was a hard-living truck driver and pipe fitter. On the side, he played a little "square dancin' guitar," as Jones puts it.

As a youngster, Jones listened to the Grand Old Opry on KRIC in Beaumont, Texas. Hank Williams, Sr., came to town in 1949 to play live on KRIC. Williams sang with Eddie and Pearl, the husband-and-wife house band that

Jones is respected by the latest generation of country stars. For example, Alan Jackson's pickup bears a sticker reading "I Love George Jones."

featured an excitable 19-year-old George Jones on electric guitar. Jones was so hyper about playing behind Williams that he never hit a note.

Jones was discharged from the U.S. Marines in 1953 and signed with the Houston-based Starday label. Throughout the 1950s, Jones enjoyed a number of rockabilly hits. In 1959, Jones had his first number-one record, "White Lightning." The hits continued in the 1960s. In the 1970s, Jones sang with artists as diverse as Johnny Paycheck, James Taylor, Ray Charles, and ex-wife Tammy Wynette.

Although the Jones-Wynette marriage was turbulent, the duet produced a string of hit singles. They became the parents of a daughter, Georgette, but in 1975, Wynette divorced Jones after seven years of marriage.

Throughout the 1970s, Jones wrestled with a drug and alcohol problem. After missing 54 concerts, he earned the nickname of "No-Show Jones." He filed for bankruptcy in

Top: Like George Foreman, George Jones hasn't let age slow him down. Jones released a new album in 1992. *Above:* Jones met his current wife at a concert in upstate New York in 1980.

1979. He tried to dry out twice, in 1979 and 1982, but was arrested for cocaine possession and public intoxication in 1983. His weight had dropped from 160 to 105 pounds.

Jones credits much of his survival to his fourth wife, Nancy Sepulveda Jones, whom he married in 1983. In March 1983, Nancy and George Jones left Nashville to open "Jones Country Music Park" near Beaumont. "It saved my life—and everything else," Jones says in a 1991 biography for MCA Records. Jones has been sober since 1986. In 1988 he was ready to put his full effort back into recording. He sold the park and moved back to Nashville.

In 1992, Jones was inducted into the CMA Hall of Fame. In October of that same year he released a new album, *Walls Can Fall.*

Wynonna Judd

Starting with "Mama He's Crazy," the Judds enjoyed a string of hits. The country music world—saddened by news of Naomi Judd's retirement—hopes Wynonna, as a solo act, can continue the line of hit songs.

Wynonna Judd battled anxiety in the early days of her solo career; she wondered if country music fans would accept her without her mother, Naomi. Wynonna's debut album, *Wynonna*, gave her a positive answer. It sold faster and in larger quantities than any previous Judd album, topping the 2 million sales mark by the fall of 1992.

Wynonna first embarked on her new career when she stepped on stage at the American Music Awards in Los Angeles on January 27, 1992. While Wynonna was onstage alone for the first time in her eight years of performing, her mother and former singing partner was in the audience.

Wynonna was born May 30, 1964, in Ashland, Kentucky, but Naomi's marriage ended in divorce. At age 12, Wynonna picked up a guitar. As she taught herself to play and sing, Naomi would add harmonies. Naomi and Wynonna continued to practice their music and eventually moved to Nashville. While there, Naomi—who had attended nursing school—looked after the daughter of record producer Brent Maher. Naomi gave him a tape of the duo. Several months later, the Judds had signed a record deal with RCA.

The mother-daughter duo enjoyed a sensationally successful career. They've had numerous number-one hits and certified gold albums. The Judds have also received every accolade possible in the music industry. Between 1984 and 1991, they were honored by the Country Music Association, the Academy of Country Music, the Music City News Country Awards, and the American Music Awards.

In late 1990, Naomi Judd announced her impending retirement due to chronic active hepatitis. The next year, the duo toured the United States as Naomi bade goodbye to her fans.

Country music lovers were relieved that Wynonna planned to continue her career. When Wynonna hit the stage at the American Music Awards, she took the first steps of what is destined to be a successful solo career.

Patty Loveless

The story of Patty Loveless is actually two stories. The first concerns a 14-year-old girl named Patty Ramey, the daughter of a Kentucky coal miner. She travels to Nashville in 1972, is befriended by Porter Wagoner and Dolly Parton, and becomes the opening act for the Wilburn Brothers. At 18, she marries the group's drummer, Terry Lovelace, and settles in North Carolina, where she spends a decade performing at hotels, fairs, and honky tonks.

The second story takes place in Nashville in 1985. A divorced Patty Lovelace impresses MCA Records executive Tony Brown with a five-song demo tape. Brown signs her and suggests she change her name; Patty Ramey Lovelace becomes Patty Loveless.

Loveless has notched hit records since 1988, and her *Honky Tonk Angel* album went gold in 1991. She has been nominated three times by the Country Music Association as Female Vocalist of the Year. In the fall of 1992, Loveless underwent successful throat surgery.

Her supple, unrestrained voice blends country rock, traditional honky tonk, and heart-stirring balladry. Loveless's strong voice is balanced by a shy stage presence that pulls an audience toward her.

Patty Loveless's voice matured during her years singing in North Carolina. Her style blends country rock, traditional honky tonk, and stirring balladry.

Loveless had lost track of the progress of country music after leaving Nashville for North Carolina. For years, she couldn't sing country music because audiences didn't want it. Then, suddenly, she started hearing requests for songs she'd never heard. "Mama He's Crazy," crowds would yell out, but Loveless was unfamiliar with the Judds. "How Blue," yelled others, but the singer hadn't heard of Reba McEntire. To investigate, she bought a few country cassettes and learned that Nashville had rediscovered the kind of music she had favored all her life.

Like Reba McEntire and Kathy Mattea before her, Loveless's climb up the ladder of success was slow, steady, and filled with enough personal growth and memorable music to gain her membership in the Grand Ole Opry.

Loretta Lynn

Although she has more country awards than any other female, timing wasn't everything for Loretta Lynn.

Loretta Webb was born April 14, 1932 or 1935 (sources differ), in Butcher Holler, Kentucky. Her father was a coal miner. At 13, she met 19-year-old O.V. "Mooney" Lynn. A month later they were married. Within a year she was alone, pregnant with her first child, while Mooney hitchhiked to Washington to find work.

Lynn relocated to Custer, Washington, where they quickly started a family. She had four of their six children before she was 21.

For her 18th birthday, Mooney bought Lynn a guitar. She taught herself to play and sat in with a local band one night. She soon became a regular. Mooney became her manager, and her first record was "I'm a Honky Tonk Girl." Mooney mailed 3,000 copies to radio stations, and some played it. Lynn then headed to Nashville. In 1961 she signed with Decca Records and joined the Grand Ole Opry.

Lynn wrote her own compositions. She had top-ten hits in 1963, 1964, and 1965, and captured the mid-1960s with songs like "Don't Come Home a-Drinkin' (With Lovin' on Your Mind)." In the 1970s, she moved to biographical songs like "Coal Miner's Daughter," which later became the title of a 1980 movie detailing Lynn's life story.

Lynn, the first female winner of the Country Music Association's Entertainer of the Year Award (in 1972), was elected to the Country Music Hall of Fame in 1988. In recent years Lynn has slowed down, partly due to health problems. She suffered her "worst heartache" in 1984 when her oldest child, Jack Benny Lynn, died.

The marriage with Mooney, however, has remained intact. They own three homes in Nashville, two in Hawaii, one in Mexico, one in the Bahamas, and a lodge in Canada.

In 1972, Lynn became the first woman to win CMA's Entertainer of the Year Award. She was elected to the Country Music Hall of Fame in 1988.

Kathy Mattea

With each successive album Mattea releases, her music grows more sparse and acoustic, her songs more earthy.

Kathy Mattea's climb to stardom was gradual. Her career finally waltzed forward in 1986 with her first top-ten hit, "Love at the Five & Dime." Three follow-ups also made the top ten. And in March 1988, "Eighteen Wheels and a Dozen Roses" spent two weeks at number one.

The youngest of three children, Mattea was born June 21, 1959, in Cross Lanes, West Virginia. Her father worked at a Monsanto chemical plant, her mother as a housewife. She took piano and tap dancing lessons and moved on to the recorder and the French horn in high school. But her musical development really began when she learned acoustic guitar so she could sing folk songs.

In 1976, as a student at West Virginia University, she hooked up with a folk group, Pennsboro. Three years later, she left for Nashville with the group's lead songwriter, Mickey Pope. Mattea teamed with Pope for a year until he returned to West Virginia. Mattea stayed on, working at the Country Music Hall of Fame as a tour guide.

She picked up jobs as a demo singer and left the Hall of Fame because she had to talk all day, which strained her voice. Instead, she found a job waiting tables near Vanderbilt University.

She soon began performing at popular nightspots, which led to a recording contract with PolyGram Records in 1983. Producer Allen Reynolds, who worked with other country singers, helped Mattea develop her own style. Her interest in distinctive songs also surfaced, and her albums introduced many new songwriters.

Mattea was named the Female Vocalist of the Year by the Country Music Association in 1989 and 1990, and she won a Grammy Award in 1991 for her vocal performance on "Where've You Been." Mattea's latest album is *Lonesome Standard Time.* In the summer of 1992, she underwent successful throat surgery.

Reba McEntire

Singer Red Steagall helped Reba McEntire get her first recording contract after hearing her sing the national anthem at the National Finals Rodeo.

Reba McEntire is the reigning queen of the new breed of performers who shook up Nashville in the 1980s.

McEntire was born in Chockie, Oklahoma, in 1954, to Jacqueline and Clark McEntire. Because her father was a champion steer roper, she and her three siblings grew up traveling the rodeo circuit. During long stretches of highway, the children learned to sing harmony.

In high school, McEntire competed in rodeos as a first-class barrel racer, but also sang with her brother and sister, performing in clubs in southeast Oklahoma. McEntire entered Southeastern Oklahoma State University in 1974 as an elementary education major, but she continued her musical career. Singer Red Steagall helped her land a recording contract.

She debuted on Mercury/PolyGram Records in 1977 with *Reba McEntire.* Newly married, she and her husband kicked off their honeymoon by visiting radio stations to promote "I Don't Want To Be a One Night Stand."

Slowly, her records entered the charts. "Three Sheets to the Wind," a duet with Jacky Ward, reached the top 20 in July 1978. Her second album, *Out of a Dream*, spawned three successful singles. She finally hit the top ten in 1980 with two songs from her *Feel the Fire* album. The following year, "I'm Not That Lonely Yet," from her album *Unlimited*, hit the top ten. By January 1983, McEntire had her first number-one hit, "Can't Even Get the Blues." A follow-up also hit number one.

McEntire changed to MCA Records where her next album, *Just a Little Love*, edged closer to rock 'n' roll than she had ever gone before.

Awards began to follow. In 1983, the Country Music Association nominated her for Female Vocalist of the Year as well as for the Horizon Award. A year later, she was named CMA's Female Vocalist of the Year, an honor she won four years in a row. McEntire was rewarded for her 1986 album, *Whoever's in New England*, with CMA's Entertainer of the Year Award. The title song also garnered her a Grammy Award for Best Female Country Vocal Performance.

Other awards included being named the Academy of Country Music's Top Female Vocalist from 1984 through 1989; she was honored as the Music City News Female Artist of the Year from 1985 through 1990; and she won the American Music Award for Favorite Female Country Vocalist from 1987 through 1989. In 1992, McEntire cohosted the CMA awards ceremony.

McEntire has dabbled in acting, with parts in *Tremors* and *Luck of the Draw: Gambler IV.*

While McEntire's career flourished, her marriage suffered. In 1987, she was divorced. In June 1989, McEntire unexpectedly married manager Narvel Blackstock. A son, Shelby, was born in February 1990.

McEntire with her son Shelby at rehearsals for the Academy of Country Music Awards.

McEntire's soulful, emotional vocal style emerged in full force on her first MCA album, *Just a Little Love.*

Tragedy struck in 1991 when her road manager and seven band members died in a plane crash. She had skipped the flight, staying behind in San Diego to shake off bronchitis. McEntire channeled her sorrows into making the album *For My Broken Heart,* a universal statement on heartbreak and sadness. Fans responded, and it was certified platinum just two months after its October 1991 release.

Lorrie Morgan

Lorrie Morgan has used her music to battle back from the tragedy of losing husband Keith Whitley to alcohol poisoning. She remarried in 1991.

Lorrie Morgan first performed at the Grand Ole Opry in 1973 at age 13. She received a standing ovation.

Morgan is the youngest child of Anna and George Morgan (a member of the Grand Ole Opry). His success had an influence on Lorrie's life. She spent two seasons at Opryland USA Theme Park, assigned to the bluegrass show. She also opened shows and sang backup for George Jones.

Morgan's first recording experience came as a teenager. While working as a songwriter and demo singer, she landed a deal with MCA Records, which released three singles in the early 1980s. Morgan was nominated as Best New Female Artist by the Academy of Country Music in 1984.

She became the youngest member of the Grand Ole Opry on June 9, 1984. Morgan was dropped from MCA's roster when she refused to cut her Opry ties.

Morgan had a daughter to support from an unsuccessful marriage, so she continued working on demo records. She met Keith Whitley while he was cutting a demo. They were married in 1986 and became parents in 1987.

The following year Morgan signed with RCA Records. She was celebrating her first album, *Leave the Light On*, when on May 9, 1989, Whitley died from alcohol poisoning.

With two children now depending on her, Morgan resumed a full tour schedule and scored her first top-ten hit, "Dear Me." Three singles from her album reached number one, and the album was certified gold in April 1990.

Studio wizardry enabled Morgan to release a duet with her late husband. The song received CMA's Vocal Event of the Year Award. Morgan was also nominated for the Horizon Award and as Female Vocalist of the Year.

The next year Morgan released her second album, *Something in Red*, which was also certified gold. In October 1992, she released her third album, *Watch Me*.

Morgan remarried in October of 1991 to Brad Thompson.

K.T. Oslin

The rise of K.T. Oslin to country stardom was unusual because she was in her mid-40s when she found success.

Born in Crossitt, Arkansas, Kay Toinette Oslin grew up in Mobile, Alabama, and Houston, Texas. As a teen, she discovered rock 'n' roll and the Texas folk music scene, and sang in a folk trio. After a varied acting career (which included a part in *Hello, Dolly* and singing jingles for commercials), Oslin developed an interest in songwriting, which attracted Elektra Records in 1981. Her first two recordings garnered little attention, however, and Elektra dropped her. But other singers liked her tunes, giving Oslin the impetus to continue.

Oslin finally got a record deal with RCA Records. Her debut single, "Wall of Tears," peaked at number 40. The video of her second single, "80's Ladies," reached number one on Country Music Television by June 1987. Two months later, the *80's Ladies* album debuted at number 15 on the *Billboard* country album charts.

That December, Oslin scored her first number-one record with "Do Ya," earning her a Grammy in February 1988. In April, she was named Top New Female Vocalist by the Academy of Country Music. In October 1988, Oslin was named Female Vocalist of the Year by the Country Music Association and was the first female songwriter to win CMA's Song of the Year Award, for "80's Ladies."

Her second album, *This Woman*, was released in August 1988. She garnered two more Grammys. Other awards followed, including Top Female Vocalist Awards from both CMA and the Academy of Country Music.

Love in a Small Town, her third album, was released in November 1990. The album showcased Oslin's songwriting talents by focusing on stories about common folk. The first single, "Come Next Monday," became an instant hit.

As a child, Oslin disliked country music because of its predominantly male point of view; now she writes songs that suit her perspective.

Dolly Parton

Dolly Parton—drawing on her humble roots for material for her songs—has risen from Tennessee poverty to wealth and glamor.

For many people, Dolly Parton *is* country music.

That's surprising, because in the 1990s Parton has become more of a pop stylist than country vocalist. And if she isn't known for pop singing, then she is recognized through numerous television and movie appearances, including a starring role in the 1980 box-office hit movie *9 to 5*.

Parton comes from some of the most unpolished roots in contemporary country music. She was born January 19, 1946, in an impoverished mountain region in Sevier County, Tennessee. Her father could not read or write.

The fourth of a dozen children, Dolly began singing as soon as she could talk. When she was eight, an uncle gave her a small Martin guitar, her first musical instrument. From that time on, Parton wanted to be a star.

Parton has never forgotten her poor roots. Some of her best-known songs reflect her early life, including "Eagle When She Flies," which she performed in dramatic fashion before President George Bush at the 1991 Country Music Association Awards at the Grand Ole Opry. Such humble material was the perfect conduit for Parton's small soprano. Her voice knew when to glitter and when to glide, which was a perfect precursor for pop crossover.

Dolly was the first member of her family to graduate from high school. The day after graduating from Sevier County High School she headed to Nashville. In 1967, she met a shy asphalt-paving contractor named Carl Dean, whom she later married.

Before her marriage, Parton lived with Bill Owens, an uncle who was a part-time songwriter. In 1966 Parton and Owens wrote a top-ten country hit for Bill Phillips. That success led Parton into her own deal with Monument Records. Her loquacious debut, *Hello, I'm Dolly*, was released in 1967. One of her first hits was "Dumb Blonde," one of the few songs she has not written or cowritten. (Parton has published more than 3,000 songs.)

The gumbo of Smoky Mountain wit, blond wigs, an impressive bosom, and long false fingernails was beginning to simmer. Country star Porter Wagoner intervened for awhile. Looking for a singer for his television and road show, Wagoner turned to Parton.

They were an immediate success, enjoying a string of hit singles. Parton left the Wagoner show in 1973, although he continued to produce her records for three more years. By 1976, Parton was looking to update her sound. She ended her long affiliation with Wagoner and signed with Gallin-Morey-Addis, a Los Angeles-based management company to help expand her horizons.

In the late 1970s, Parton released three albums that went gold. By the 1980s, a polished sound had evolved, but it still had a country charm. Parton had surrounded herself with lush, upbeat pop arrangements and contemporary rock musicians.

In the fall of 1990, Parton received an honorary degree from Carson-Newman College in Jefferson City, Tennessee. She brought down the house at the commencement ceremonies when she called herself "Dr. D.D.," as a reference to her married name, Dolly Dean, as well as her bust size.

Above: For a brief time in the mid-1960s, Parton leaned toward pop music, but she soon returned to country. *Below:* Parton entertained the audience at the 1992 Country Music Association Awards.

Kenny Rogers

By the time Kenny Rogers arrived in Nashville, he had nearly two decades of diverse experience as an entertainer.

More than once, Kenny Rogers had zoomed toward the top ring of music stardom, only to have it slip away. When he arrived in Nashville in the mid-1970s, he was too broke to hire his own band. To pay bills, he appeared in television commercials for mail-order guitar lessons.

Born in Houston in 1938, Rogers was 20 years old when he first tasted success with "That Crazy Feeling," earning him an appearance on *American Bandstand.* When he failed to have a follow-up hit, he took a job in a Houston jazz trio and then in a Las Vegas lounge band. He joined the New Christy Minstrels in 1966. When that group broke up, he and three other members formed the First Edition. With Rogers as lead singer, the group recorded several hits, including "Ruby, Don't Take Your Love to Town."

In Nashville, Rogers gained another chance when he signed a contract with United Artists Records. With his smooth, romantic style and husky tenor, he forged a formula that proved highly popular. His second album included the hit "Lucille," which earned Rogers his first Grammy and his first awards from the Country Music Association. When he released "The Gambler" the following year, Rogers used its success to reach heights rarely achieved by a country music entertainer.

Between 1977 and 1983, Rogers racked up more than $250 million in album sales. He appeared in several TV specials and movies, including the highly rated *The Gambler.* In 1983, RCA Records lured him to sign a recording contract with a hefty bonus. By 1990, Rogers had won three Grammys, 18 American Music Awards, five Country Music Association Awards, and eight Academy of Country Music Awards.

By the time he signed with Reprise Records in 1990, his hit-making streak had tapered off. After little success at Reprise, he moved to Giant Records in the fall of 1992.

Ricky Van Shelton

Ricky Van Shelton was once a rock 'n' roll fan with no desire to be a country singer. But after older brother Ronnie asked Shelton to play a gig with his bluegrass band, Shelton was hooked.

Shelton and his wife, Bettye, left Grit, Virginia, for Nashville so Shelton could pursue his dream of becoming a country music star. Through a coworker of Bettye's, Shelton got in touch with Rick Blackburn, head of CBS Records, who heard Shelton in 1986.

After years of no attention, Shelton's career took off. Within two weeks he was recording his first album, *Wild-Eyed Dream.* "Crime of Passion" was its first single, and it soared into the top ten. Many number-one records followed. He appeared on the Grand Ole Opry in June 1987.

The awards followed. In 1988 he was named Top New Male Vocalist by the Academy of Country Music, the Music City News Star of Tomorrow, and the Country Music Association's Horizon Award winner. Shelton also became a member of the Grand Ole Opry that year. Just eight weeks after the release of his second album, *Loving Proof,* Shelton had another gold album to add to his collection.

Shelton has dominated the fan-voted awards in recent years. In 1989, he claimed three TNN Viewers Choice trophies and four Music City News awards. When TNN and Music City News combined awards shows in 1990, fans voted him both Male Vocalist and Entertainer of the Year. The following year, he won the same awards.

Shelton's third album, *RVS III,* continued the same mix of honky tonk and rockabilly and produced four top-five hits. It was certified platinum.

In 1991, Shelton released *Backroads.* "Rockin' Years" became a chart-topper, accompanied by a music video named Country Music Television's number-one video of 1991.

Ricky Van Shelton's rich, powerful voice earned him an encore at the Grand Ole Opry in 1987—a rare occurrence on the Opry stage.

Ricky Skaggs

Ricky Skaggs served an impressive apprenticeship before recording his own music for a major record company. He quickly proved he'd learned his lessons well, creating 16 top-ten hits between 1980 and 1986 with a fresh sound that updated bluegrass and honky-tonk music. His success pointed country music in a new direction and set the stage for the new stars of recent years.

Skaggs was born July 18, 1954, in Cordell, Kentucky. By age five, his father was giving him mandolin lessons, and his mother was teaching him traditional mountain songs. At age seven, he performed on a TV show hosted by Flatt & Scruggs. At age 15, he joined the band headed by Ralph Stanley. In 1972, at age 17, he recorded an album with childhood friend Keith Whitley, a member of Stanley's band.

Ricky Skaggs's first Nashville record, *Waitin' for the Sun To Shine,* surprised country music executives, topping 500,000 in sales within a year.

He spent the mid-1970s as a member of several highly acclaimed bluegrass bands. Emmylou Harris recruited him to join her Hot Band in the late 1970s, and Skaggs began recording solo albums for an independent label, Sugar Hill Records.

Skaggs's independent recordings set the stage for his first Nashville album for Epic Records. *Waitin' for the Sun To Shine* earned Skaggs his first Country Music Association honors. The young singer was named Male Vocalist of the Year and also won the Horizon Award. In 1985 Skaggs was given country music's most prestigious annual honor: He was named Entertainer of the Year by the Country Music Association. He went on to win Grammys in 1984, 1985, and 1986, and he shared the 1987 Vocal Duo of the Year Award with his wife, Sharon White.

Of his role in revitalizing country music in the 1980s Skaggs says: "I set out to create a more traditional, back-to-basics kind of sound. . . . It was something I felt like the fans wanted, and it was certainly something I wanted."

Although some of Doug Stone's best-known songs may be rather melancholy, offstage he's a witty, personable ball of energy.

Doug Stone

Doug Stone's musical memories go back as far as he can remember. A family snapshot captures three-year-old Doug sitting entranced in front of a record player. At age seven, his mother took him to a Loretta Lynn concert.

At 16, the Georgia native quit school, bought a mobile home with money he had earned performing, and built a portable studio. Thus began more than a decade of performing in hotel lounges and late-night honky tonks in the Atlanta area. By the mid-1980s, tired of the grind, Stone returned to his hometown of Newnan, Georgia.

Stone—whose real name is Doug Brooks—went to work as a diesel mechanic. He limited his music performances to weekends at the local VFW lodge, where aspiring manager Phyllis Bennett spotted him one night. Bennett introduced the singer to Doug Johnson, a producer who recorded three songs Stone had written. When former Epic Records executive Bob Montgomery heard Stone's work, he offered him a contract.

Garth Brooks had just released his debut album, so Epic executives convinced Doug Brooks to change his name. At the time, Doug was writing a song titled "Heart of Stone," and it provided his stage name. In the spring of 1990, Stone debuted with "I'd Be Better Off (In a Pine Box)," which earned him a Grammy nomination in 1991. His albums, *Doug Stone* and *I Thought It Was You*, have both been certified gold.

Born June 19, 1956, the singer has four children, two of whom reside in Newnan, Georgia, with Stone and his third wife, Keri. His parents divorced when Doug was 12. His four brothers and one sister were raised by his father.

"I've had a lot of experience in life, and I think that helps my songs," Stone says. "If you can draw on your experiences, then you get closer to the truth. That's what country music is about: The truth."

Marty Stuart

Marty Stuart has been in the music business since he was 12 years old, when he toured with a gospel-bluegrass band.

Marty Stuart likes to say he earned his high-school diploma as a mandolin player in Lester Flatt's band and his university degree as lead guitarist in Johnny Cash's band. Stuart grew up in Philadelphia, Mississippi; at age 13, he was recruited by Lester Flatt after the singer had split from partner Earl Scruggs. After Flatt's death, Stuart hooked up with Johnny Cash, performing with him until 1985.

All along, Stuart knew he wanted to create his own music. He released two independent albums, *Marty: With a Little Help from His Friends* and the acclaimed *Busy Bee Cafe*. In 1986, he joined CBS Records and put out *Marty Stuart*. But CBS and Stuart disagreed on musical direction, so Stuart went elsewhere.

In 1989, he emerged on MCA Records with *Hillbilly Rock*, an album that took a fresh perspective on indigenous American music by delving into the roots where country and rock 'n' roll intertwine. The album provided several radio hits.

By that time, Stuart had developed an individual stage style built upon a collection of some 200 pieces of flashy cowboy clothes, including dozens of jackets and shirts with special embroidery and rhinestone-studded patterns. He wanted to update the colorful western-styled attire of such country legends as Hank Snow, Porter Wagoner, and Webb Pierce.

Stuart continued to write prolifically while establishing his own singing career, and his songs were recorded by such diverse performers as Emmylou Harris, Buck Owens, and Jann Browne. Travis Tritt invited Stuart to join him in a duet of "The Whiskey Ain't Workin'." The song helped earn Stuart and Tritt the 1992 CMA Vocal Event of the Year Award.

Stuart's next album, *Tempted*, kept the momentum of *Hillbilly Rock* rolling forward. The record allowed Stuart to reveal his talent for bluegrass and gospel as well as expanding on his country-rock style.

Pam Tillis

In 1992, Pam Tillis—nominated for CMA's Horizon Award—entertained the audience at the awards ceremony.

Pam Tillis has been around country music for quite some time. The daughter of Mel Tillis, she appeared with him on the Grand Old Opry when she was eight years old. During her musical career, she experimented with pop, rock, new wave, disco, and jazz before returning to her roots in country music.

For years Tillis refused to listen to those who told her she was destined to follow in her father's footsteps. The tales about her sleeping in her daddy's guitar case at a recording studio are true, but she claims he was never around long enough to teach her how to play the instrument.

At 16, Tillis was in a car accident that severely disfigured her face, requiring years of surgery. She eventually dropped out of the University of Tennessee, moved to San Francisco, and formed a jazz-rock combo that became popular in the Bay area. She married, then returned to Nashville, where her son, Ben, was born. Three weeks after his birth, she broke up with her husband.

Tillis earned a living as a session singer and songwriter. She dreamed of a rock 'n' roll career, though she continued to experiment with different musical styles. She fronted a rhythm and blues band for a while and recorded songs that showed the influence of disco and new wave.

Following a trip to England in the mid-1980s, Tillis returned to Nashville, intent on exploring her country heritage. She began making waves with a string of solid singles. Songs penned by Tillis were recorded by various country artists.

Signed to Arista Records in 1990, Tillis finally claimed her place as a country performer with the release of *Put Yourself in My Place*. She was nominated for the Country Music Association's Horizon Award in 1992. Her latest album, *Homeward Looking Angel*, was released in September 1992.

Randy Travis

Minnie Pearl once said of Randy Travis: "A voice like his only comes along once in a generation." That voice helped turn country music around.

Minnie Pearl, country music's famous humorist, called Randy Travis "a new vehicle with old wheels." She meant he sounded good, looked good, and was moving country music into the future by relying on past musical styles.

But Travis paid his dues. The second of six children, he was born Randy Traywick on May 4, 1959, in Marshville, North Carolina. His father bred horses, raised turkeys, and managed a small construction firm. His mother sorted potholders in a fabric mill.

At age eight, Travis learned chords on a guitar. Two years later, his father grouped his four sons into a country harmony act known as the Traywick Brothers.

Travis veered into trouble in his teens. He dropped out of ninth grade and got into scrapes with the police. In his final brush with the law, he was arrested for breaking and entering, a felony.

Before his court date, Travis won a talent contest at Country Music City USA, Charlotte's preeminent country music honky tonk owned by Lib Hatcher. She inquired about his life, and with his parents' consent, appealed to the court to put him on probation and in her care. Travis moved in with Hatcher and her husband and took over as Country Music City USA's vocalist.

In 1978, singer Joe Stampley produced a handful of Travis's songs on Paula Records and took tapes of the songs back to Nashville. But no one showed any interest.

Hatcher, now divorced, and her protégé weren't giving up. In 1980, the two moved to Nashville. She talked her way into a job managing Nashville Palace, a music club and restaurant across from the Opryland Hotel. Travis went to work with her, mopping floors and flipping hamburgers. He also sang when he could, performing under his new stage name, Randy Ray. He eventually worked himself into a full-time slot.

In 1985 Martha Sharp, Warner Bros. Records top talent executive, listened to Travis sing and decided to sign him. Kyle Lehning, who had worked with Ronnie Milsap, produced most of *Storms of Life* (two songs were produced by Keith Stegall). Before putting out the album, however, Warner Bros. wanted to test the reaction of listeners. The first single, "On the Other Hand," was disappointing, climbing to only 68 on the country charts. The next song, "1982," fared better, making the top ten. Warner Bros. gave "On the Other Hand" another chance; it reached number one. *Storms of Life* spent 12 weeks at the top of the charts.

His second album, *Always & Forever*, spawned four consecutive number-one songs and spent 10 months atop the country album sales chart.

Travis dominated many awards shows in the late 1980s, winning more than 40 honors in his first four years, including a Grammy for Best Country Vocal Performance by a Male and several awards from the Country Music Association and the Academy of Country Music. His albums *Old 8 × 10*, *No Holdin' Back*, and *Heroes and Friends* extended his million-selling streak into the 1990s. In 1991, Travis starred in a special on HBO with George Jones.

Top: Randy Travis pulls in as much as $10 million annually from concerts. *Bottom:* Travis and Lib Hatcher were married in a ceremony in Hawaii in 1991.

Travis Tritt

While Travis Tritt is aware of country music traditions, he has not linked himself with such "new traditionalists" as Randy Travis.

Travis Tritt burst on the country music scene in late 1989 with his first single, "Country Club."

Born February 9, 1963, in Marietta, Georgia, Tritt grew up on his family's 40-acre farm. His father also worked several side jobs. Tritt's mother encouraged her son to sing in their church's children's choir.

Tritt taught himself to play guitar when he was only eight years old. At 14, he was songwriting. His father tried to discourage his musical aspirations, but Tritt pressed on and their relationship turned rocky.

For four years, Tritt supported himself by working at a heating and air conditioning firm. But a talk with his boss convinced him to give music a shot. So for six months, Tritt worked days and performed nights. When he quit his job, his father stopped speaking to him.

By 1984, Tritt was making a meager living as a club act across Georgia. Tritt's first marriage lasted less than two years, but Tritt remarried. Wife Jodi Barnett acted as his manager, consultant, and booking agent. They divorced in 1989.

Tritt's break came in 1984 when he met Danny Davenport, a local pop promotion man for Warner Bros. Records. Over the next two years, they worked together and recorded an album. In 1988, Tritt signed with Warner Bros. with Ken Kragen as his manager.

Tritt's debut album, *Country Club*, helped him snag the Country Music Association's Horizon Award in 1991, which mended his relationship with his parents. That same year, Tritt and Marty Stuart recorded a rowdy single together that climbed to the top of the charts and earned them the 1992 CMA Vocal Event of the Year Award.

It's All About To Change, the singer's second album, was also certified platinum. Tritt's latest album, *T-R-O-U-B-L-E*, was released in August 1992 and topped 500,000 in sales in the first month. Also in 1992, Tritt received a high honor: he became a member of the Grand Ole Opry.

Tanya Tucker

Tanya Tucker roared into country music like a Texas tornado in 1972. While some considered her success at age 13 a head start, Tucker didn't. She knew she wanted a music career when she was eight years old.

Born in Seminole, Texas, her parents Juanita and Beau (now her manager) encouraged her musical aspirations. They even arranged her audition for the 1972 movie *Jeremiah Johnson*. She landed a small role.

After the family relocated to Henderson, Nevada, Beau financed a demo tape that reached producer Billy Sherrill, who signed Tucker to Columbia Records. Tucker herself picked the material for her debut album. "Delta Dawn" was her first hit record.

By her 16th birthday, Tucker had a string of top-ten albums and singles. But she had also gained a reputation for hard living. Cancelling several concert dates in 1978, Tucker repackaged herself in spandex for her *TNT* album, which pushed her toward rock 'n' roll. Although the record was a best-seller, the move backfired and her career fizzled.

By 1982, Tucker was broke. She released two solid country singles that became top-ten hits. Following a three-year break from recording, Tucker signed with Capitol Records in 1986 and was back on top with her 1987 album, *Love Me Like You Used To.* Singles from the album resulted in two 1988 Country Music Association nominations.

Tucker made headlines in 1989 when she gave birth to a daughter, Presley Tanita (named after Elvis Presley), and announced her intention to remain unmarried.

Also in 1989, she released *Strong Enough to Bend; Tennessee Woman* followed in 1990. Her 1991 album, *What Do I Do with Me*, was another hit. Tucker's latest album, *Can't Run from Yourself*, was released in the fall of 1992.

On October 2, 1991, Tucker was a double winner, giving birth to a son, Beau Grayson, hours before being named CMA's Female Vocalist of the Year.

Tanya Tucker has always had a good amount of sex appeal to go along with her distinctive, melodic vocals.

Conway Twitty

Conway Twitty is a rare bird. He has never received an award as a solo artist from the Country Music Association. (He won four as a duet with Loretta Lynn.) He is rarely seen on television and shies away from print interviews. In a departure from country tradition, Twitty rarely speaks on stage.

But as a solo act, Twitty has had 63 top-ten hits on the *Billboard* country charts.

Twitty was born Harold Jenkins on September 1, 1933, in Friars Point, Mississippi.

If Conway Twitty had not made it big in music, he could have gone into baseball. The military draft derailed a career with the Philadelphia Phillies.

Young Harold was exposed to the primitive guitars and raw harmonica of rural blues. Twitty maintains the blues made more of a difference in his development than listening to the Grand Ole Opry.

Twitty was five years old when he began playing guitar, picking up songs from his father. During his teens, Twitty's family moved to Helena, Arkansas. There, Twitty formed the Phillips County Ramblers, a country-blues band that landed a weekly gig on KFFA radio.

After being discharged from the Army in 1957, Twitty followed the Sun: particularly the rockabilly sound that was coming out of Sun Studios in Memphis. Although Sun owner Sam Phillips got Twitty in the studio, he was unhappy with the results. Nothing was released.

Twitty found a manager who encouraged him to continue to follow the path of rock 'n' roll. The manager also suggested a snazzier stage name, so Twitty turned to a map. He found Conway, Arkansas, and Twitty, Texas.

In 1958 Twitty scored his biggest hit, "It's Only Make Believe." The song soared to number one on the pop charts. He continued to sing penitent pop ballads until 1965, when he crossed over to country. Twitty's early 1970s success in dueting with Loretta Lynn gave him added credibility. Twitty still charms his audiences with a cunning country flutter in his restrained baritone.

Trisha Yearwood

One of Trisha Yearwood's trademarks is her choice of songs: She tends to pass over songs about "weak women" who forgive too easily.

Late in the 1980s, when Garth Brooks and Trisha Yearwood worked as Nashville demo singers, Brooks promised Yearwood that if he got a break in the recording industry, he would try to help her. She made a similar pledge. By 1991, Garth Brooks was a star. When he learned Yearwood had signed with MCA Records, he set her up with his management team and invited her to accompany him on tour as his opening act.

Yearwood's first hit, "She's in Love with the Boy," didn't need much assistance. The song pushed its way to number one on the country music charts. Her album, *Trisha Yearwood*, was released in July 1991 and has sold more than a million copies Her second album is titled *Heart in Armor*.

Trisha Yearwood grew up in Monticello, Georgia, a village of about 2,000 some 60 miles from Atlanta. As a youngster, she loved records by Elvis Presley and Linda Ronstadt. Her first performance experiences came in high school musicals and choral groups.

While at the University of Georgia, Yearwood realized her heart belonged to music. She transferred to Nashville's Belmont University and enrolled in its music business curriculum. While working toward her degree, she had an internship at MTM Records. After graduation, she went back to the firm as a receptionist. Besides sharpening her understanding of the music industry, the work brought her in contact with many of the industry's key players.

Despite being warned about a supposed industry and public bias against female country music performers, Yearwood choose songs that presented a strong woman's point of view. "That's What I Like About You," a song originally written for a male singer, is typical of Yearwood's musical choices.

Concert audiences applaud Yearwood's expressive voice. She received an enthusiastic ovation after a power failure at one appearance forced her to sing her encore number a cappella.

Hank Williams, Jr.

Hank Williams, Jr., performed his first concert at the tender age of eight, recorded his first song at 14, and scored his first number-one country song at 16. But the young man who had changed his name from Randall Hank Williams to Hank Williams, Jr., was quite aware he was riding the coattails of his legendary father.

Hank, Jr. spent the 1960s performing his father's songs and adhering to his mother's career direction. In 1974, Williams decided to step out of his father's shadow and stand on his own. Against the wishes of his mother, he moved from Nashville to Cullman, Alabama, and began an album that combined Southern rock, Delta blues, and rebel country.

The influence of Williams's introduction of a rock sound to country music can be heard in such acts as the Kentucky HeadHunters and Travis Tritt.

The landmark album *Hank Williams & Friends* was a bold departure for Williams. Its rock edges alienated Williams from the Nashville establishment and from his longtime record company, MGM Records. In 1977, Williams released *The New South*, a pointed statement about his vision of a new musical style. Produced by Waylon Jennings, *The New South* was Williams's first album after joining the new record company established by music industry mogul Mike Curb.

Williams closed the 1970s by setting personal sales records. He released the *Family Tradition* album in April and followed it with *Whiskey Bent and Hellbound* in October. Both albums topped 500,000 in sales within a year. Thirty years after his birth on May 26, 1949, in Shreveport, Louisiana, Williams had succeeded in forging his own identity.

By 1982, Williams had attracted a fanatically loyal following. In concert, he regularly drew crowds of 10,000 or more, a rarity for a country music artist at that time. Williams continued to pull in those numbers for the remainder of the decade. By the end of the 1980s, Williams's total sales topped the $25 million mark.

Despite his success, Williams was shunned by the

When Williams received a Video of the Year Award from the CMA, he quipped, "You know, I make a little audio, too."

Hank Williams, Jr., with his fourth wife, Mary Jane Thomas.

country music awards organizations. He was viewed as more of an outsider than even country outlaws Waylon Jennings and Willie Nelson.

Eventually, the country music industry began to come around. In 1985, Williams received a Video of the Year Award from the Country Music Association. Two years later, Williams began to gain the recognition that seemed so long overdue. The Academy of Country Music named him Entertainer of the Year. A few months later, the CMA granted him their version of that same honor. Williams continued to be honored in 1988, 1989, and 1990 by various music associations, including his first Grammy in 1990.

The singer continues to be an avid outdoorsman, retreating for a period each year to a 300-acre spread in Montana to fish and hunt big game. He even moved his business office to Paris, Tennessee, which is located in an area suitable for outdoor recreation.

During the 1990s, Williams has continued to change and grow. In 1990, he married his fourth wife, Mary Jane Thomas. The following year, he terminated several long-running business associations when he switched his concert bookings to the William Morris Agency and signed a multiyear contract with Capricorn Records.

The Southwest The Western Beat

Rodeos are connected with country music both directly and indirectly. Several country music stars are former competitors.

Nashville may be about turning country music into a tightly controlled business, but the Southwest is about keeping the music freewheeling. The country music of the Southwest covers a wide spectrum. It includes everything from the country blues of Jimmie Rodgers to the swing of Bob Wills and the Texas Playboys to the honky tonk of Ernest Tubb. Also part of the Southwest are the hard country sounds of Buck Owens and Merle Haggard, the country rock of Emmylou Harris, and the progressive style of the Austin scene represented by Lyle Lovett.

The thread that ties them all together is a legacy of innovations and new trends. Jimmie Rodgers brought a bluesy syncopation and jazzy swing to country music. Swing bands introduced drums, horn sections, and electric and steel guitars. They also proved that country music could fill a dance floor. Honky-tonk pioneers such as Al Dexter stripped down the big band sound of swing to a sparse, hard-driving music that maintained the beat and increased the emotional content of the lyrics. Their music gained national prominence in the hands of Tubb, Hank Williams, and others.

As Nashville secured its status as the capital of country in the late 1950s and early 1960s, the only serious challenge arose from Bakersfield, California. Located about 100 miles northeast of Los Angeles, Bakersfield was a center for transplanted Oklahomans and Texans who had migrated west to escape the impoverished conditions brought on by the Depression. These job seekers

In Austin, Texas, musical independence is supported and the integrity of the song reigns supreme. Sixth Street (above) is the city's musical nerve center.

had brought with them their love for honky-tonk music.

Wynn Stewart and Tommy Collins were the first two singers from Bakersfield to enjoy national success, but it was the crackling sounds of Buck Owens that became best-known. Merle Haggard experienced a more enduring success than Owens. Haggard's early recordings belie a strong Bakersfield influence, but he would go on to create music that bore no allegiance to any regional sound.

The Bakersfield musicians would influence an unlikely group of young performers who settled in Southern California. The genesis of West Coast country rock came with the union of Gram Parsons and the Byrds on the classic album, *Sweethearts of the Rodeo.* Groups who grew out of this alliance or who were influenced by it include the Flying Burrito Brothers, Linda Ronstadt, the Eagles, and Emmylou Harris. This progressive sound would prove influential in Nashville and in the country music youth movement of the 1980s and 1990s.

Bakersfield, California, is tied to country music more than any other western city. The County Museum (above) celebrates the city's rich connection to country music history.

Meanwhile, a ragtag group of musicians with a country-tinged sound began congregating in Austin, Texas. Blue-collar country fans, urban folkies, and aging hippies found a common ground in the progressive country music of Willie Nelson, Jerry Jeff Walker, and others. This group valued strong lyrics, instrumental virtuosity, and musical diversity.

The music of the Southwest has mirrored the character of the people who originally settled in the region. It's a sound that values individualism, freedom, physical activity, and spiritual reflection. Over the years, it has repeatedly injected vitality into country-western music.

Asleep at the Wheel

The leader hails from Pennsylvania. The band was formed in West Virginia and came into its own in the San Francisco Bay area. But in 1974, when Asleep at the Wheel pulled into Austin, Texas, the western swing band found its spiritual center. Ever since, the hardest-working band in country music history has called Texas home.

Six-foot, six-inch Ray Benson is the lone remaining original member of Asleep at the Wheel. Since forming in 1970, the band has seen more than 70 members. They have put out at least 13 albums on eight different record labels, winning three Grammy Awards.

Asleep at the Wheel has remained true to the music they love, and they've managed to build up a loyal following.

But their spirited, sometimes comic Texas swing music has never found acceptance on radio. So, Asleep at the Wheel has rolled along for more than two decades, never quite achieving star status.

Nevertheless, the Wheel keeps moving, playing more than 200 shows a year. "We play a wide range of music, really, but very little of it is in the mainstream," Benson says. "Trying to sell our music is a record company nightmare. We ain't easy, as far as pigeonholing goes. But I don't like trends. Period. So we just do what we do. I'm proud of Asleep at the Wheel because we've existed against the odds. I'm happy that we've stuck around, and we've been able to maintain a certain level of success just playing what we love."

Benson formed Asleep at the Wheel with vocalist/songwriter Leroy Preston and steel guitarist Lucky Oceans in West Virginia. Shortly afterward, the band moved to San Francisco. They moved to Austin just as that city was beginning to build a reputation as a significant music center that paid little attention to commercial trends.

Outside of the band, Benson has produced an album for songwriter Darden Smith and an acclaimed duet by Rob Wasserman and Aaron Neville. He has costarred with Dolly Parton in a television movie, *Wild Texas Wind*, and he has worked on movie sound tracks for Robert Duvall and Willie Nelson.

Some of Nanci Griffith's independent albums on Rounder Records sold better than many better promoted albums put out by major labels.

Nanci Griffith

Nanci Griffith performed at a rowdy Austin nightclub called The Hole in the Wall in the early 1970s. "It was the toughest bar you could play," she says. "You could always hear the pinball machine in the backroom, and there was always a bar fight around 1:15. That's where I developed my vocal style. I had to sing in a way that got their attention." She instilled an aggressive edge to her voice and more tempo into her folk songs.

Griffith was born and raised in Austin, Texas. When she was ten years old, Griffith met Carolyn Hester, a Los Angeles folk singer, and they began corresponding. By the time she was 14, Griffith was performing in local clubs, chaperoned by her father.

Her style drew attention from fans but seemed too idiosyncratic to mainstream record companies. So Griffith put out her own albums and toured regularly, appearing throughout the South and East Coast.

After five albums, Griffith signed a contract with MCA in 1986. That same year, Kathy Mattea took Griffith's "Love at the Five & Dime" into country music's top ten. Her first three MCA albums sold decently despite a cold shoulder from country radio. Her Nashville recordings made her a major star in Ireland.

"What I do is very different," she says. "I know what I do is not mainstream or a repetition of anything that has been done. You have to create your own road, and my road has been going out and touring America and creating a following. It was that following that brought me a record contract."

In 1988, she shifted her recording base from Nashville to Los Angeles. After experimenting with a lusher, moodier sound on *Storms* and *Late Night Grande Hotel*, she returned to Nashville to record an album exploring her folk roots, *Other Voices, Other Rooms.*

Merle Haggard

Anyone who divides country music into old and new traditions is missing a critical point, one that Merle Haggard has hung his cowboy hat on for his entire career.

Haggard's greatest challenge has been to redefine tradition, and it's worked. Haggard has had more than 30 number-one country hits. He has been nominated more than 40 times for Country Music Association Awards, more than any other male country entertainer.

Haggard was born on April 6, 1937, in Bakersfield, California. His father had a low-paying job for the Santa Fe Railroad, which left a lasting impression on Merle. To this day, Haggard travels in a tour bus that carries the Santa Fe logo.

Haggard was nine years old when his father died, and he grew rebellious as he got older.

Merle Haggard has rolled up some impressive numbers: 43 CMA award nominations, which is more than any other male country performer, and 38 number-one country singles.

He started hopping short-line trains and at the same time first heard the liberating yodel of Jimmie Rodgers.

Between 1957 and 1960, Haggard did time in San Quentin on a burglary conviction. He repatterned his life in the prison textile mill. Upon his release, Haggard returned to Bakersfield and began playing the country music he had learned in prison.

From the first time he walked on a stage, Haggard's style has been impossible to define. Along with The Strangers, his innovative nine-piece band, Haggard has always played a kaleidoscope of pop, swing, blues, and what he terms country jazz.

Offstage, Haggard represents a stubborn loyalty to American self-reliance. One anecdote best illustrates his independence. He was supposed to appear on the first worldwide telecast of *The Ed Sullivan Show.*

"Minnie Pearl, Jeannie C. Riley, and I were booked," Haggard said. "They had me in for the part of Curly in Rodgers and Hammerstein's *Oklahoma!* So I learned all that stuff and sung all them songs. As the week progressed, and we got closer to the time of broadcast, they kept working these dance steps in for me. Now, I told them at the beginning, I don't dance, I don't do choreography, and that I don't want to.

"Well, they just kept shoving a little more dance and a little more choreography and pretty soon I was dancing around this big set with each of

Lyle Lovett

Lyle Lovett likes to toy with conventions. He's a Texan who's afraid of cows. He's touted as a country singer-songwriter, but he's just as likely to play honking blues, swinging jazz, or somber folk music.

Lovett uses his quirky views on life and love as his calling card. Though he hasn't achieved broad radio airplay, his three albums on MCA have sold well. His artistic standing was underlined when his second album, *Pontiac*, earned him a Grammy in 1989.

Lovett grew up in Klein, Texas, on the same plot of land where his great great grandfather, town namesake Adam Klein, first settled. Today, Lovett lives in a home once owned by his late grandfather.

Lovett began singing and writing songs while earning degrees in journalism and German at Texas A&M. He met singer-songwriter Nanci Griffith by interviewing her for the school paper. With her support, he started playing small nightclubs in Houston, Dallas, and Austin. At a folk festival in Luxembourg in 1983, Lovett met the J. David Sloan Band and followed them back to Arizona. Using the Sloan band, Lovett recorded his first songs in Scottsdale.

Lovett took the tape to Nashville, where he received such encouragement that he returned to Arizona to record 14 more originals. Songwriter Guy Clark passed Lovett's new music to Tony Brown of MCA Records. Brown added a few instrumental parts to ten of Lovett's songs and released them in 1986 as *Lyle Lovett.*

The first album revealed a singer-songwriter with a refined, assured vision and a witty way with words. He expanded his versatility in *Pontiac* and fully displayed his ability to blend jazz, blues, and country on his third album, *Lyle Lovett and His Large Band.*

By the early 1990s, Lovett had contributed songs to several movie soundtracks. His fourth album, *Joshua Judges Ruth*, was released in March 1992.

Lyle Lovett's fourth album, *Joshua Judges Ruth*, explores jazz, gospel, blues, and swing, as well as country.

Willie Nelson

Willie Nelson had logged nearly three decades as a professional musician when he returned to his native state of Texas in the early 1970s. He had spent the 1960s fighting the Nashville system, and it wasn't until he retreated to Austin that he finally found the audience and the inspiration he needed to make music the way he wanted it to be heard.

Many in the industry consider Willie Nelson the best songwriter in country music.

Nelson was born April 30, 1933, in Abbott, Texas. When he was very young, his parents divorced, and he was raised by his grandparents. After graduating from Abbott High in 1951, Nelson spent less than a year in the Air Force before attending Baylor University. He worked selling vacuum cleaners and Bibles door-to-door to pay for his schooling. After two years, Nelson left college and became a disc jockey. Nelson cut his first record in 1957 while working at KVAN radio in Vancouver; he pressed 500 copies of "No Place for Me" (an original composition) and sold them for a dollar each. Today, this single is regarded as Nelson's rarest recording.

Nelson returned to Texas in 1958 but felt he was going nowhere fast. Two years later, he moved to Nashville. He was hired in 1961 as a bass player for Ray Price's band, the Cherokee Cowboys. Offstage, Nelson's songwriting began to blossom. He penned such songs as "Crazy," performed by Patsy Cline, and "Hello Walls," performed by Faron Young. Nelson signed with Liberty Records in 1962.

By 1964, Nelson was a Grand Ole Opry regular. Through the rest of the 1960s he enjoyed moderate success. However, he was becoming increasingly disenchanted with the lush strings and emotive backing choirs that were defining the Nashville sound.

Nelson's commercial break came with a 1974 switch to Columbia Records, which gave him complete artistic control. His debut album at Columbia, *Red-Headed Stranger*, was a smash and included a top-ten hit. In 1976, Nelson followed up with *Wanted: The Outlaws*, which combined him with Waylon Jennings, Jessie Colter, and Tompall Glaser. The album hit number one on the country charts and crossed over into the top ten on the pop charts.

Nelson has also branched into movies. He had a major role in the 1979 film *The Electric Horseman* and co-starred with Dyan Cannon in the 1980 film *Honeysuckle Rose*. He has also devoted considerable time to the Farm Aid movement.

Nelson has received many honors, including five Grammy awards, eight Country Music Association awards and the

Despite his own troubles with the I.R.S., Nelson manages to find plenty of time for Farm Aid.

Even after decades in the music business, Nelson still loves to tour; he's on the road more than 200 days a year.

National Academy of Popular Music Lifetime Achievement Award.

The 1990s began ominously for the singer with the outlaw image. In late 1990, the Internal Revenue Service seized Nelson's property for payment of $16.7 million in back taxes. Two homes and many personal items were auctioned off, and Nelson recorded a mail-order album, *The I.R.S. Tapes*, to pay the debt.

Nelson also experienced tragedy. On Christmas Day 1991, his only son, Billy, committed suicide at the age of 33. But Nelson's show will remain on the road. His storied life has been about bending but never breaking.

Buck Owens

Although Buck Owens has retired, his music will influence country music for years to come.

Buck Owens started singing in the clubs of Bakersfield, California, where bands had to project over the roar of the patrons. The experience showed that an audience came alive when a prominent drum beat was paired with an electric guitar. This energized blend of traditional country and rock 'n' roll percussion can be heard in the country-rock sounds of today.

Owens was born Alvin Edgar Owens on August 12, 1929, in Sherman, Texas. His father moved the family to Mees, Arizona, when Owens was eight years old. At 22, Owens moved to Bakersfield, California, to form his first band, the Schoolhouse Playboys.

Owens played with the Schoolhouse Playboys between 1951 and 1958 in Bakersfield. The Schoolhouse Playboys were more of a rockabilly outfit than a country band, which is how Owens was attracted to the drums.

Bakersfield was the perfect environment for experimentalists such as Owens. The invigorating, jazzy strain of country music became more expressive and less repressed than if the band had been playing in slick, manufactured Nashville.

Owens left the Schoolhouse Playboys in 1957 to join the Tommy Collins Band. In 1958, Owens was signed by Capitol Records; by 1959, the band had their first hit. In 1962, Owens formed his own group, the Buckaroos.

Owens was cohost of the popular *Hee Haw* television series between 1969 and 1986. His cornball television image overshadowed his unique musical contributions.

In the summer of 1991, Owens said he was retiring after a concert in Texas. Owens has made wise business investments over the years. He owns a television station and two radio stations in Bakersfield and two radio stations in Phoenix. Owens also owns several magazines and printing presses in Bakersfield.

Owens spends his leisure time playing golf, and he is active in numerous Southern California charity events.

Will Buck ever be back?

With Buck Owens, one never knows.

George Strait

When George Strait first visited Nashville in 1979, he was told his music was behind the times. By the end of the 1980s, Nashville was singing a different tune. In the decade following *Strait Country*, the Texan's 1981 debut album, he racked up 25 number-one songs and 11 gold albums. Twice he has received the Country Music Association's Entertainer of the Year Award.

Strait was born May 18, 1952. His father was a junior-high math teacher and part-time rancher in Pearsall, Texas. Strait's initial musical experience was singing rock songs with a band of high-school buddies.

Strait enlisted in the Army in 1971. A year later, while serving in Hawaii, he taught himself to play guitar by studying a Hank Williams songbook. Before long, the base commander recruited the young Texan to lead a country band. During his last year of service, Strait mainly performed country music on military bases.

Returning home, he enrolled at Southwest Texas State University in San Marcos. On campus, he advertised himself as a singer looking for a country band. A group named Ace in the Hole called. With Strait as lead singer, the band began performing nightly.

In 1979, Strait received a bachelor's degree in agriculture and started managing the family ranch. After working all day on the ranch, he'd sing with Ace in the Hole. That same year, he signed with MCA Records and had a top-ten hit from his debut album, *Strait Country*.

Strait has enjoyed much success since that debut album. For example, *Ocean Front Property* opened at number one on *Billboard*'s country album chart. In 1992, he had the starring role in *Pure Country;* the sound track was a big hit on the pop charts. But amid all the success, Strait has also faced tragedy. His 13-year-old daughter, Jennifer, was killed in a 1986 auto accident.

George Strait almost gave up his dream of country music stardom, but his wife persuaded him to give it one more shot. Soon he signed with MCA Records and was on his way.

The Texas Tornados

Only a state as big as Texas could conjure something as bawdy as the Texas Tornados. Members Freddie Fender, Doug Sahm, Augie Meyers, and Flaco Jimenez offer an irresistibly eclectic mixture of country music, conjunto (the accordion offering lead melody against a polka backbeat), and rhythm and blues.

Freddie Fender grew up in the Rio Grande valley border town of San Benito. He is the best-known singer in the band, having scored with such hits as 1959's "Wasted Days and Wasted Nights" (re-recorded and sent to number one in 1975), the 1974 ballad "Before the Next Teardrop Falls," and the lilting 1976 hit, "You'll Lose a Good Thing."

Fender worked with vocalist Doug Sahm as early as 1959 at a sock hop in Sahm's hometown of San Antonio and again in the 1970s. The name Texas Tornados is derived from a nickname once bestowed on Sahm, a veteran of the 1960s rock band the Sir Douglas Quintet.

Blues-inspired organist Augie Meyers learned his minimalist four-beat style from bluesman Jimmy Reed, and contributed to "Mendocino" and other hits by the Sir Douglas Quintet. Flaco Jimenez's conjunto accordion playing is practically legendary.

The Texas Tornados first got together in late 1989 at Slim's, a San Francisco nightclub owned by rock singer Boz Scaggs. Warner Bros. was attracted to the idea of a Tex-Mex version of the Traveling Wilburys and signed the Tornados.

"Soy De San Luis," a track from the group's self-titled debut album, won a 1990 Grammy for Best Mexican-American Performance. A follow-up recording, *Zone Of Our Own*, received a 1991 Grammy nomination for Best Country Performance by a Duo or Group with Vocal. The band's third album, *Hangin' on by a Thread*, was released in November 1992.

The Texas Tornados, left to right: Flaco Jimenez, Augie Meyers, Doug Sahm, and Freddie Fender. Their Tex-Mex blend of country and conjunto is difficult to classify.

Dwight Yoakam

Dwight Yoakam's first album was funded by $5,000 raised by the singer and his producer, Pete Anderson.

Dwight Yoakam has a country boy's background, a college intellectual's vocabulary, and a Southern California angle. Yoakam roared his way into country music with his first album, *Guitars, Cadillacs, Etc., Etc.* The first song, a remake of Johnny Horton's "Honky Tonk Man," established Yoakam. But Yoakam's outspoken criticism of the Nashville music industry caused a stir.

Yoakam comes from independent stock. He was born October 23, 1956, in Pike Floyd Hollow in the Kentucky hills. When Yoakam was an infant, his parents, David and Ruth Ann, moved 90 miles north to Columbus, Ohio. His father worked at a Texaco station, and both parents were ridiculed for their hill-country accents and rural expressions.

On most weekends, his family traveled back to Kentucky to visit relatives. Yoakam has vivid memories, both powerful and comforting, of his Kentucky heritage.

Yoakam wrote his first song at age eight. By 1976, a year out of high school, he was performing throughout the Ohio River valley. Two years later, he arrived in Nashville, ready to dedicate himself to the style of music he loved. But he was told he was "too country."

Rather than compromise, Yoakam moved to Los Angeles. He rented a one-room apartment, slept on a mattress on the floor, and drove an airport freight van by day while singing in the working-class honky tonks of suburban L.A. at night.

Four years later, he met Pete Anderson, an educated young man dedicated to the raw, traditional forms of American music. Before long, other Los Angeles-based, roots-music advocates took an interest in Yoakam's brand of country. He and his band began opening for such Southern California favorites as Los Lobos, the Blasters, and X.

Nashville finally noticed. With Anderson as his producer, Yoakam's first two albums on Reprise Records sold 1.5 million copies in two years.

The Western Beatniks

Joe Ely's rockin' country style has earned him tours with the likes of Tom Petty, Linda Ronstadt, and the Rolling Stones.

Jerry Jeff Walker concedes it's not easy to explain why Texas seems to encourage a certain kind of rugged, romantic songwriting style.

"Texans celebrate their own lifestyle a lot," says Walker, a New Yorker who settled in Austin in the early 1970s. "Texans like to write songs about their boots, their hats, their way of life. They write about things they know and things that matter to them. It's been a part of the Texan music tradition forever."

Walker was among those who inspired such Texas talents as Guy Clark, Joe Ely, Billy Joe Shaver, Butch Hancock, and Townes Van Zandt. Recently, some music critics have referred to these musicians as the Western Beat.

In the late 1960s, Walker roamed America, using his thumb for transportation and his guitar for street-corner income. When Walker stopped in Austin, "it was the first place I'd been where people didn't think I was crazy for wanting to sing songs with just my guitar," he says.

Walker sings romanticized tales of the road and the troubadour's lifestyle in a frayed, world-weary voice.

Walker fostered many up-and-coming Texas songwriters, including Guy Clark. Clark was born in 1941 in Monahans, Texas, and, as a young adult, he started performing in Houston.

In 1970, he moved to Los Angeles. Nine months later, he signed a songwriting deal with a music publishing company. His new bosses encouraged him to move to Nashville, which he did in 1971.

Though Clark's commercial success has been minimal, his influence is more extensive. His songs are best known in versions by other singers. Lyle Lovett and Nanci Griffith are among those who cite him as inspiration.

Another influential group of Texans first surfaced in Lubbock. One band, the Flatlanders, featured three young men—Joe Ely, Butch Hancock, and Jimmie Dale Gilmore—who would later become seminal Texas musical figures. The Flatlanders recorded one album that received scant public recognition.

Ely grew up in Amarillo, moving to Lubbock at 12. Before finishing high school, he had taken to the road, carrying his guitar with him. He spent time in New York and Europe before work with a circus brought him home to Lubbock. After hooking up with the Flatlanders, Ely migrated to Austin.

His debut album in 1977 was widely hailed for its distinctive distillation of honky tonk, rockabilly, Mexican folk music, and American blues. He has since forged a new, individualized style of rockin' country music.

Ely also drew on the songs of his old partners, Gilmore and Hancock. Gilmore dropped from the musical landscape after the Flatlanders went their separate ways. He returned in 1988 with *Fair & Square.* Of the Flatlanders, Gilmore most closely sticks to traditional country music in his arrangements and themes. Gilmore's songs tend to describe common experiences with a poetic slant and a hint of mysticism.

Hancock is best-known for the songs he writes for others. Ely has filled his albums with Hancock songs for years. A Lubbock native, Hancock's songs are closely tied to the landscapes of the wide-open Texas plains. He captures the romanticism of the landscape and conjures up the howl of the wind and the mystery of the seemingly endless horizon.

Top: Jimmy Dale Gilmore's music combines the bluesy simplicity of Jimmie Rodgers with the honky-tonk twang of Webb Pierce. *Above:* Jerry Jeff Walker was one of the first national stars to emerge out of the fruitful Austin music scene.

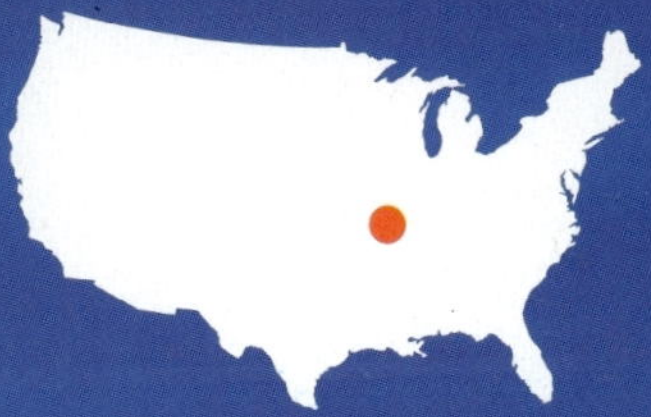

Branson, Missouri Ozark Mountain Hot Spot

Opposite: Visitors originally flocked to the scenic Ozark Mountains for its breathtaking beauty. *This page:* Music theaters soon sprouted to entertain the travelers. The theaters have expanded beyond Branson to such Ozark outposts as Eureka Springs, Arkansas, home of the Ozark Mountain Hoe-down Music Theater.

Roy Clark visited Branson, Missouri, for the first time in the late 1970s. What he found amazed him. Hordes of middle-class Americans flocked to this small town in the Ozark Mountains to see old-time country music entertainers in shows put on daily. The shows featured such acts as the Baldknobbers, the Foggy River Boys, the Presleys, and the Plummers—performers whose names were virtually unknown beyond Branson.

Clark figured a performer with a national reputation—such as himself—might provide a slicker alternative to the established vaudeville-style shows. If successful, it would eliminate some of the need to constantly be on the road. In 1983, Roy Clark's Celebrity Theater opened, Branson's biggest showroom at the time. It was an immediate success.

Clark's peers took notice. In 1986, Grand Ole Opry performer Boxcar Willie opened a 900-seat theater in Branson. It drew capacity crowds twice a day from April to December. Moe Bandy, Danny Davis, and Ray Price soon followed.

Then, in 1990, Mel Tillis opened a 2,000-seat showroom. It too was packed daily. When Tillis earned several million dollars his first year, the dam broke. Suddenly, it seemed every veteran country star was announcing plans to open a Branson theater.

By 1991, Branson's list of performers included Mickey Gilley, Jim Stafford, Ray Stevens, and Cristy Lane. The following year, Johnny Cash, Willie Nelson, Andy Williams, Glen Campbell, Louise Mandrell, the Gatlin Brothers, Johnny Paycheck, Jeanne Pruett, and Buck Trent moved

The Grand Palace, one of Branson's newest and grandest showplaces, seats 4,000. Glen Campbell and Louise Mandrell are the Palace's primary headliners.

into town. Wayne Newton and Kenny Rogers also announced plans to open elaborate entertainment palaces.

Branson quickly turned into a boomtown, and the patrons marched to a country music beat. A town with a population of 3,700 hosted approximately five million visitors in 1992. As of 1992, Branson had around 30 theaters with nearly 50,000 seats.

The numbers seem even more phenomenal since the heavy season lasts only six months. "In July," according to Boxcar Willie, "it might take you more than an hour to drive a mile down Highway 76, what with the thousands of cars and all, but in January, you can shoot a cannon down the street and no one would notice. There's hardly a soul in sight here in the winter."

Decades ago, people traveled to the Branson region to camp and fish. In the late 1950s, dams were built on the river, creating a sporting paradise. Soon, word about the great fishing lured many anglers. Since these enthusiasts often brought their families, entrepreneurs developed entertainment for adults and children. In 1960, a retiree from Indiana bought some land that included a well-explored cave on the city limits of Branson. He built an entertainment complex with an Old West theme, offered space to crafts people, and called it Silver Dollar City.

At about the same time, a dramatic play based on *Shepherd of the Hills*, a popular religious book by Harold Bell Wright, opened nearby. *Shepherd of the Hills* became a popular option for evening entertainment. With more and more family-style attractions, anglers found it easier to persuade their families to vacation in this remote spot.

The first regular musical performances in the area coincided with this expansion in tourist-related activities. The Mabe brothers began entertaining local crowds in the late 1950s. The brothers, along with sister Marge Blansit, combined traditional mountain string music with gospel quartet singing and cornball comedy.

When the *Shepherd of the Hills* began its nightly performances, the Mabe brothers were hired to provide music for a square dance scene. The group they portrayed was known as the Baldknobbers, a vigilante group that roamed the Ozarks during the Civil War. The brothers retained the name when they began supplementing their role in the play with regular performances at Silver Dollar City.

Before long, the Mabes started staging their own Baldknobbers show in down-

Shoji Tabuchi, a native of Japan, fell in love with country music in the 1960s. He has been one of Branson's most popular entertainers.

town Branson. The theater held 50 people, and if fewer than 12 customers showed, that night's performance was canceled—an occurrence that happened often in the early days.

The Baldknobbers kept moving, always looking for a better location. In 1965, the brothers bought an old skating rink on the banks of Lake Taneycomo. Three years later, the Mabes bought four acres on Highway 76 and built their own 860-seat theater. The brothers have since expanded it to accommodate twice as many customers.

Though the Baldknobbers were Branson's first regular professional musical performance act, they weren't the first musical group to locate on the Highway 76 strip. The Presley Mountain Music Jubilee, operated by another family of musicians with deep roots in the performance community of the Ozarks, moved into its present location on Highway 76 in 1967, a year before the Baldknobbers' theater opened.

Lloyd Presley had performed on a radio show in Springfield, Missouri, in his youth. By the late 1950s, he appeared periodically at the White River Co-op meetings in Branson. In 1961, Lloyd and his sons, Gary, Lloyd, and Steve, began performing regularly at Fantastic Caverns, one of the caves near Branson. When the Presleys (no relation to Elvis) first opened their theater on Highway 76, it featured 250 folding chairs. By 1981,

The Shepherd of the Hills Tower provides a great view of the Ozarks. A dramatization of the popular religious book, *Shepherd of the Hills*, has been staged nightly at this spot for more than 30 years.

Presleys' Mountain Music Jubilee Theater was the first showplace in Branson to feature more than 2,000 seats. By that time, the show's lineup included Gary's sons, Scott, Greg, and Eric.

The Baldknobbers and the Presleys continue to perform daily on Highway 76, providing a tie to Branson's formative style of old-time, Ozarks-flavored entertainment. Though the names on the marquees down the street now flash some of the best-known names in show business, the emphasis remains the same as when the Mabes and Presleys first set up folding chairs in town.

Branson was built and continues to prosper because it presents wholesome, family-style entertainment in a safe, down-home setting. The rooms are budget priced, and the food is dished out in heaping servings in buffet lines at low prices. The strongest beverage on tap in the theaters is Mountain Dew, the language never gets any more profane than an occasional reference to cow manure, and nearly every establishment is empty by ten in the evening.

Branson is a glitzy entertainment capital unclouded by gambling or drinking, and many of the town's entertainers are hitting the jackpot daily.

Moe Bandy

While Moe Bandy watched the walls go up on his 900-seat Americana Theater in Branson in 1991, he told the construction workers a story. Eighteen years earlier, Bandy had hocked his furniture for $900 to pay for a recording session. At the time, he had been leading a double life: working full-time as a sheet metal worker by day and leading a band through honky-tonk hits at night. Bandy had recorded before—putting out country music singles in Texas since 1964—but he had little to show for his efforts. The $900 session introduced him to Nashville producer Ray Baker. A few months later, Baker called Bandy and said he had a song for him. This time, Bandy took out a personal loan, and the gamble paid off. Bandy recorded "I Just Started Hatin' Cheatin' Songs Today." It went on to become one of the surprise hits of 1974. Bandy was 30 years old when he finally reached the national charts.

Although Moe Bandy had been making records since 1964, it wasn't until 1974 that he finally had a hit.

Born in Meridian, Mississippi, Bandy was obsessed with music and rodeo as he grew up. He competed in rodeos throughout his teens. When he turned to music, he drew on his rodeo experiences in such hits as "Rodeo Romeo" and "Cowboys Ain't Supposed to Cry."

For most of the 1970s, Bandy enjoyed moderate success as a traditional honky-tonk singer. In 1979, Bandy joined another country veteran, Joe Stampley, to create several successful duets. The duo's initial single, "Just Good Ol' Boys," became Bandy's first number-one single. Bandy and Stampley were named Vocal Duo of the Year by the Country Music Association in 1980 and by the Academy of Country Music in 1980 and 1981.

Bandy began performing regularly in Branson in the mid-1980s before settling into his own Americana Theater on Highway 76. He has built a home in the Ozarks that he shares with Margaret, his wife of 28 years.

Nashville record executives didn't see much potential in Boxcar Willie, but he has sold more than a million records.

Boxcar Willie

Boxcar Willie was born in 1975 when Lecil Martin watched John Denver win the Entertainer of the Year Award from the Country Music Association. Martin, who was then 44 years old, had been a fan of traditional country music since childhood; he was disgusted that the CMA's highest annual award was given to Denver. To Martin, it represented how country music was being overtaken by pop trends and rock 'n' roll performers.

Martin, born in Sterratt, Texas, had been a country music performer as a youngster, but he gave it up while in his 20s. In the ensuing years, he toiled as a disc jockey, an airplane pilot, a flight instructor, a refrigerator repairman, and an auto mechanic. Following the 1975 CMA Awards, he decided to return to country music. He donned a ragged coat, overalls, and a beat-up hat. Calling himself Boxcar Willie, the singing hobo, he dedicated himself to reviving traditional country songs.

Five years later, Boxcar Willie made his debut on the Grand Ole Opry. Music publisher Wesley Rose had seen Boxcar Willie perform at a British country music festival, and the music executive invited the singer to come to Nashville and meet his business partner, Roy Acuff. Boxcar Willie, thanks to Acuff's invitation, performed a medley of train songs on the Opry and received a standing ovation.

Around the same time, Boxcar Willie began selling albums through television commercials. Nashville record executives had refused to put his albums out: They didn't see much promise in a middle-aged former DJ who dressed like a bum. But Boxcar Willie sold more than a million albums within a few years. Boxcar Willie's latest album is *Rocky Box*. At age 50, he was named the Most Promising Male Vocalist at the Music City News Awards.

Boxcar Willie was among the first stars to follow Roy Clark into Branson. He opened the 900-seat Boxcar Willie Theater in 1987.

Glen Campbell and Louise Mandrell

Glen Campbell is a veteran entertainer of more than 30 years: from session musician to TV show host to big-screen movies.

By 1967, Glen Campbell had spent seven years in Los Angeles. As a musician, his career was going wonderfully. He had played guitar on albums by Elvis Presley and Frank Sinatra and had also been part of the studio group for Phil Spector's famed Wall of Sound. A native of Delight, Arkansas, Campbell enjoyed a minor hit in 1962 with the Green River Boys. But five years later, nothing had happened for him as a lead performer or singer.

Campbell was 31 years old in 1967 when he visited John Hartford in Nashville. After returning to L.A., Campbell recorded Hartford's song, "Gentle on My Mind." Campbell's follow-up, "By the Time I Get to Phoenix," proved to be an even bigger hit. When Campbell won four Grammys—two as a country vocalist and two as a pop performer—his stardom was secured. He was named Entertainer of the Year by the Country Music Association in 1968.

Campbell has characterized his style as "crock," a word he invented to describe a blend of country and rock. His sweet tenor and dynamic arrangements come from pop music; the strong storylines and good-natured image are drawn from country.

In the late 1960s, Campbell was involved in various video endeavors. He hosted his own variety series on CBS. Campbell made his big-screen debut in *True Grit* and then costarred in another movie, *Norwood.* Despite two big hits, Campbell's success slowed in the 1970s, and he began making periodic appearances in Branson in the late 1980s.

Louise Mandrell was 15 years old when her older sister, Barbara, signed a recording contract with Columbia Records. When Barbara put together a band that year for a concert tour, she hired Louise to play bass.

Louise Mandrell was born July 13, 1954, in Corpus Christi, Texas. Younger than Barbara, Louise acquired her sister's interest in music and ability to play several instruments. As a member of the Do-Rites, Louise was featured on fiddle as well as bass. By the time she graduated from high school, she had traveled more than 400,000 miles as a road musician. Eventually, Grand Ole Opry star Stu Phillips offered Mandrell an opportunity to enjoy more of the spotlight. With Phillips, Mandrell opened each concert with several songs before stepping back to take a featured spot in his band. From there, she took a similar role for Merle Haggard, giving her the chance to open concerts for one of country music's biggest stars.

In 1977, Mandrell decided to move center stage. She quit the road and signed with Columbia Records. Her initial work received little attention, except for a duet with R.C. Bannon in 1979, and it wasn't until 1983, two years after switching to RCA Records, that she finally enjoyed her first top-ten hit, "Save Me." Other hits followed.

Though Mandrell's recording success lasted only a few years, her popularity as a performer has proved more durable. A high-energy entertainer, her concerts often have more in common with a Las Vegas variety show than a laid-back country affair.

In 1992, Campbell and Mandrell began sharing headlining chores at the Grand Palace, a 4,000-seat showroom operated by the Silver Dollar City theme park.

Louise Mandrell got her start playing in older sister Barbara's band. She now shares billing at Branson with Glen Campbell.

Campbell describes his music as "crock," a blend of country and rock.

Johnny Cash

Johnny Cash is a big man who tends to do things in a big way. The Man In Black has secured more pop hits than any other country artist, and only George Jones has enjoyed more country music chart hits. Cash has been a movie actor, a best-selling author, and a host of a successful TV series. So it makes sense that when Cash decided to come to Branson, the move would include three music theaters, a musical theme park, a hotel, and a horse arena, among other things.

Johnny Cash's songs about the concerns of the common man are a reflection of his own impoverished childhood.

Cash was born February 26, 1932, into an impoverished farm family in Kingsland, Arkansas. The Cash family entertained themselves with music, with everyone joining in. Cash began writing songs by the time he reached high school.

After graduation, Cash moved to Pontiac, Michigan, to work in a Fisher Body plant. Bored there, he joined the U.S. Air Force and spent four years in Germany. While there, he taught himself to play guitar. His first performances were for crowds of soldiers on foreign military bases.

When he returned to the States, he settled in Memphis. He met two musicians, guitarist Luther Perkins and bassist Marshall Grant, and began performing informally with them. He talked them into auditioning at Sun Records. Sun owner Sam Phillips was intrigued and asked Cash to come up with something with a rock beat. The singer went

home and wrote "Cry Cry Cry," which became his first country music hit in 1955.

Cash's initial songs featured the singular Cash sound: A walking bass and a simple, deep-toned, single-note guitar that provided primitive backing. In search of a stark sound, Cash purposely omitted the fiddles and steel guitars that rang out on most country music of the period.

In 1956, Cash joined the Grand Ole Opry. Two years later, he signed with Columbia Records. His second Columbia single, "Don't Take Your Guns to Town," sold a half-million copies and continued Cash's run of success on both the country and pop charts.

In the 1960s, Cash descended into a well-documented period of drug use. By his own account, he cleaned himself up with the support of singer June Carter and became a born-again Christian along the way. The couple married in 1967. His new bride and her mother, country star Maybelle Carter, were regular guests on the ABC-TV series *The Johnny Cash Show*, which ran from 1969 to 1971. The show led to a career revival that resulted in several hit songs while the show was on the air.

Top: Cash is more than just a crossover to rock: He was inducted into the Rock 'n' Roll Hall of Fame. *Above:* Wife June Carter often performs with Cash when he tours.

Cash has sold more than 50 million records and won seven Grammy Awards. His skill as a songwriter is similarly impressive. He's received 23 citations from the song-tracking agency BMI for radio airplay. In 1980, Cash became the youngest person inducted into the Country Music Hall of Fame.

The legendary singer underwent heart bypass surgery in February 1989, but by the spring of that year he was performing regularly again. In 1992, Cash continued to record and maintained a touring schedule that called for more than 150 concerts a year.

Roy Clark

Roy Clark's long tenure with *Hee Haw* kept him in the public eye but obscured his great talent as a musician.

Onstage and on screen, Roy Clark tends to emphasize his grinnin' as well as his pickin'. His broad smile and lighthearted jokes are as much a part of his popularity as his outstanding talent as a guitar and banjo player. But behind that smile is a canny businessman with a history of making the right move at the right time.

In 1969, he agreed to cohost a comedy program known as *Hee Haw*, and he stayed with the show after it ventured into syndication. Then, in 1983, he became the first country star to open a theater in Branson. At the time, it was considered a gamble since the Ozark town was home to only about ten shows, all led by local acts.

Clark was born April 15, 1933, in Meaherrin, Virginia. His first instrument was the banjo. By the time Clark was eight years old, he had appeared on the stage of the Grand Ole Opry by winning regional banjo competitions.

Clark got his first recording contract in 1962 with Capitol Records after spending three years as a crack session player behind rockabilly star Wanda Jackson. After his first hit record, in 1963, Clark drifted off into television. He never came back. Clark was already fast friends with country television star Jimmy Dean, but after his hit records, he appeared on *The Tonight Show*, *The Andy Williams Show*, *The Mitzi Gaynor Special*, *Sammy and Company*, and even dropped in for a cameo on *The Odd Couple* comedy series. One of the highlights of Clark's recording career was *Makin' Music*, a swinging mid-1970s MCA album that paired Clark with Texas bluesman Clarence "Gatemouth" Brown.

Today, Clark tours occasionally, performs at his own theater in Branson, Missouri, and earns a nice income from *Hee Haw* syndication.

The Gatlin Brothers

The Gatlin Brothers made a startling announcement in June 1991: Larry, Steve, and Rudy Gatlin were planning on retiring from touring and recording. Larry was to undergo surgery on his vocal cords, and the road had become expensive and tiresome.

But Branson presented the brothers with the opportunity to perform in a quality theater without traveling, and Larry's surgery proved successful. So, less than a year after planning their retirement, the Gatlins announced they would perform regularly at their own Branson entertainment complex.

Larry was born in May 1948 in Seminole, Texas. Steve followed in April 1951, and Rudy in August 1952. The brothers first performed at a talent contest, which they won, when Larry was six years old.

While attending the University of Houston, Larry auditioned for a gospel quartet. He didn't get the job, but the group later asked him to fill in during a Las Vegas engagement backing Jimmy Dean. The opening act—Dottie West—heard Gatlin sing a few of his own compositions backstage. She recorded two of them on her next album and sponsored Larry's move to Nashville.

Gatlin soon signed a contract with Monument Records. His albums were issued under his name, though his brothers sang harmonies. When they signed with Columbia Records in 1979, the billing changed to Larry Gatlin and The Gatlin Brothers Band. By that time, Larry had already won a Grammy for his first top-five single, "Broken Lady."

The trio enjoyed several hits, but the senior Gatlin later said the group squandered their potential by becoming involved with drugs and alcohol. They abandoned those habits in 1985 when all three became born-again Christians.

"The Branson situation for us is just perfect," Larry Gatlin tells *Country Song Roundup.* "We get to see the people, we get to sing our music, we get to make a little money, and we get to be at home with our families."

The Gatlins had pretty much decided to stop touring in 1991, but Branson has made it possible for them to continue to play.

Mickey Gilley

As a youth, Mickey Gilley used to trade piano tips with cousin Jerry Lee Lewis, who inspired Gilley to a musical career.

When country music star Mickey Gilley followed Roy Clark into Branson, he had already shown a canny sense for keeping ahead of country music trends. That's not bad for someone who entered show business as a second thought and whose first hit was a recording done as a favor.

Born March 9, 1936, in Natchez, Louisiana, Gilley spent much of his youth with his cousins, Jerry Lee Lewis and Jimmy Swaggart. They traded tips on playing piano, but only Lewis talked of a music career. In 1956, after Gilley had moved to Houston and started working with an engineering firm, he heard Lewis's first hit, "Crazy Arms." When Lewis came through town with lots of money, Gilley began to think of music differently.

For 20 years, Gilley recorded for small, independent companies. He enjoyed some regional hits, but little national success. By 1974, he had built a following in Houston with his own nightspot, Gilley's Club, and a traditional, honky-tonk performing style. A concession worker at Gilley's suggested he record her favorite song, "She Called Me Baby." On the flip side, Gilley added "Room Full of Roses," which became his first number-one country hit.

Gilley's initial hits emphasized steel guitar, honky-tonk piano, and bluesy vocals, all of which went against the prevalent Nashville sound. But sparse honky tonk was soon staging a comeback in Nashville.

Gilley and his club played a primary role in the movie *Urban Cowboy*, which led to other acting roles, including guest spots in several television shows.

After several pop-flavored hits in the 1980s, Gilley decided to move his operation to Branson. "Branson works because it provides the best conditions for both the fans and the entertainers," Gilley explained. "It's a high-quality situation for everyone involved." The singer opened a restaurant in Branson in 1992.

Cristy Lane

During the 1960s, Cristy Lane was a housewife in Peoria, Illinois, who loved to serenade her family while working around the house. She would sing the classic country hits she learned as a child, the gospel standards she heard in church, and the contemporary hits played on the radio. Her husband, Lee Stoller, repeatedly praised her singing and encouraged her to get beyond her shyness when they entertained friends at home. The compliments of friends led Stoller to believe his wife's voice rated with nationally known performers.

Lane began performing in clubs in 1968 and eventually moved to Nashville in 1972. Stoller formed a record label, LS Records, to release his wife's music. Lane had a string of hits that continued into the early 1980s.

Then, Stoller, a businessman known for his marketing skills, decided to take Lane's music directly to the American people. Stoller had heard how Slim Whitman, a country music veteran who could no longer find support in Nashville, had sold more than a million copies of a greatest-hits album by advertising on TV.

Cristy Lane and her husband, Lee Stoller, have built a following that has sold millions of albums.

Stoller arranged a recording session that featured Lane singing gospel and country classics. He then bought massive amounts of air time on cable channels to show commercials. The ads featured his wife singing as titles of her recorded songs rolled across the screen. The album sold in monumental numbers; within a few years, Lane reportedly sold more than 20 million albums through direct marketing on television and in print.

In the late 1980s, Lane began performing periodically in Branson at the Starlite Theater and other venues. She now performs regularly at the 1,300-seat Cristy Lane Theater.

Johnny Paycheck

Johnny Paycheck's best-known hit, the Grammy Award-winning "Take This Job and Shove It," seemed to reflect the singer's opinion of his career. Paycheck would often appear to be on the brink of major stardom, then he would sabotage his progress with self-destructive behavior. His problems culminated in 1986, when he received a prison sentence for shooting a man. However, the governor commuted Paycheck's sentence in 1991, and the singer emerged a new man. While in prison, he earned his high school diploma, quit smoking, and joined programs to end his alcohol and drug addictions.

Born Donald Lytle in Ohio on May 31, 1941, Paycheck first recorded as Donnie Young in 1959 before changing his name in the mid-1960s. By then, he had played in many of country music's greatest bands. As a songwriter, he contributed to the success of other country music stars. Paycheck scored hits of his own as early as 1965. But his work appeared on small, independent record labels because his reputation kept the major labels away. Finally, Epic Records agreed to give Paycheck a chance—if he cleaned up his act.

Working with Epic Records producer Billy Sherrill, Paycheck enjoyed an occasional hit in the early and mid-1970s. Then "Take This Job and Shove It" became his first and only number-one hit. Success proved short-lived. In the 1980s, Paycheck's behavior grew more erratic, an inclination reflected in some of his songs, including "Drinkin' and Drivin'" and "Armed and Crazy."

Once out of prison, Paycheck said, "When you get a chance to reevaluate yourself like that, it can do a world of good. I now have a totally positive feeling about myself."

In 1992, Paycheck began to appear regularly in Branson in a theater that once featured a local act, the Foggy River Boys. The theater seats 1,000 people and is located on Highway 76.

Johnny Paycheck lived an erratic lifestyle that culminated in a prison term. While in prison, he turned his life around.

Jim Stafford's music comes from a mixture of musical and songwriting talent combined with offbeat humor.

Jim Stafford

Jim Stafford has often said he came from a family of pickers. His parents and grandparents grew up in Tennessee, where they picked guitars, banjos, and mandolins. Stafford was raised in Eloise, Florida, where he and his relatives picked oranges, lemons, and grapefruit.

Stafford is a talented instrumentalist and songwriter whose greatest fame has come from his humorous ditties, including popular hits, "Spiders and Snakes," "Wildwood Weed," and "My Girl Bill."

Born January 16, 1944, Stafford joined his first rock group at 14 and switched to country music at 21. After two years in Nashville, he moved to Atlanta, where his work in an exotic dance club led to his blending his oddball humor into songs to draw laughs from patrons.

Stafford's comic flair soon found favor in songwriter clubs along the eastern seaboard, and he became a popular attraction at the Bitter End in New York, the Cellar Door in Washington, Mr. Kelly's in Chicago, and other nightspots. His friend Kent LaVoie, who performed under the name Lobo, introduced Stafford to MGM Records head Mike Curb, who signed the witty songwriter to a recording contract. His second single, "Spiders and Snakes," sold more than a million copies in 1973.

Stafford scored all his hits within a two-year period following "Spiders and Snakes." But his career as a performer flourished, appearing on stages in Las Vegas and Atlantic City and on television programs.

By the late 1970s, he also had made his TV acting debut. His first role was on *The Love Boat.* He hosted a 1979 syndicated TV special, *Jim Stafford's Grand Central,* and in the early 1980s he was cohost of ABC-TV's *Those Amazing Animals.*

Stafford began performing in Branson regularly when he took over his own 800-seat theater in 1991.

Ray Stevens

Some of Ray Stevens's better-known hits include "Ahab the Arab," "Gitarzan," and "The Streak."

Ray Stevens says he *thinks* funny. A multifaceted entertainer, Stevens is best-known for his comical musical stories that use absurd characters to poke fun at social issues and lifestyle trends. Stevens has also been a top record producer and arranger for other artists, and his own hits have varied from a universal pop classic ("Everything Is Beautiful") to biting commentary ("Mr. Businessman"). Besides writing and performing, he runs his own music publishing company in Nashville.

"I've always liked to try whatever came to mind," Stevens says, explaining the variety of his musical output. "I sometimes have thought that maybe I should have concentrated more on this area or that area of entertaining. But I didn't. I've always liked to try something unusual to see how it would come out."

Born January 24, 1939, in Clarksdale, Georgia, Stevens was a child prodigy on the piano and was headed toward a classical music career when he formed a rhythm-and-blues band in high school. One of his early singles, "Sergeant Preston of the Yukon," sold more than 200,000 copies before a lawsuit brought by owners of the radio program of the same name forced the record to be withdrawn. The following year, Stevens was back with a bigger hit, "Jeremiah Peabody's PolyUnsaturated Quick Dissolving Fast Acting Pleasant Tasting Green and Purple Pills."

In recent years, Stevens has focused more on performing than at any time in the past. Since opening the Ray Stevens Theater in Branson in 1991, he has drawn an average of 3,000 people a day through the summer months.

"It's a fantastic place," he says of Branson. "Playing six days a week can be a real tough schedule, but I have learned to pace myself well. And it's a great place to play. The people are great; it's a real cross-section of America."

Mel Tillis

Mel Tillis has never minced words about his stuttering. Ever since he caught malaria as a three year old in Pahokee, Florida, Tillis has stuttered. But as fans of his Branson concerts can attest, he has made the affliction work for him. Tillis often uses stuttering as comic relief during performances. An early 1980s album was called "M-M-Mel Live," and he even titled his 1985 autobiography *Stutterin' Boy.*

But Tillis's real gift is his ability to articulate a blend of country shuffle and classic pop melody. Among his 500 compositions are Kenny Rogers's hit "Ruby, Don't Take Your Love to Town" and "Detroit City," which was a hit for Bobby Bare.

As "Ruby, Don't Take Your Love to Town" (the story of an impotent Vietnam veteran begging his wife to stay with him) shows, Tillis doesn't shy away from challenging subject matter. Tillis's lesser known "Commercial Affection" deals with prostitution.

Tillis was born August 8, 1932, in Pahokee, Florida. He learned guitar as a child but didn't play professionally until 1956, when he dropped out of the University of Florida. His first composition, "I'm Tired," was a number-one hit for Webb Pierce. Tillis went on to have regional success with "The Violet and the Rose" and "Georgia Blues," recorded for Columbia Records, his first label.

While Tillis was known as a songwriter in his early years in Nashville, his commercial break came with a gruff baritone reading of the Harlan Howard classic "Life Turned Her That Way." Tillis was named Entertainer of the Year in 1976 by the Country Music Association. Later, he coproduced and costarred in the 1985 film *Uphill All the Way* with Roy Clark.

His daughter is country singer Pam Tillis, who has enjoyed success on the country charts in the late 1980s and 1990s. In 1991, Mel Tillis opened his own theater in Branson (to order tickets, just dial 335-MMEL).

Mel Tillis—whose daughter is Pam Tillis—often uses his stuttering to great comic effect during his concerts.

Buck Trent

In concert, Buck Trent—a gifted instrumentalist—is the personification of pickin' and grinnin'.

Buck Trent came to prominence in the early 1960s for two reasons: He was a featured instrumentalist on the television program *The Porter Wagoner Show*, and he was the first musician to effectively electrify the five-string banjo.

Both achievements represent important aspects of Trent's career: He is an innovative instrumentalist who is aware of the value of entertaining an audience. Unlike many other exceptional musicians, he doesn't try to capture an audience by dazzling them with technique. Trent prizes showmanship as much as musicianship.

Born in 1938 in Spartanburg, South Carolina, Trent took to stringed instruments early. At age 8, he was playing the steel guitar, his favorite instrument until he discovered a banjo in his grandfather's attic.

In 1960, Trent debuted at the Grand Ole Opry as a member of Bill Carlisle's band. His expertise attracted several offers to tour and to record, and he eventually hooked up with Wagoner.

Trent always sought to add new dimensions to the banjo. Earl Scruggs's virtuosity on the traditional five-string banjo had already elevated the instrument's capabilities to dizzying heights. Rather than new fingering techniques, Trent tried to expand the sounds the banjo could produce.

Trent likes to tinker, and he has invented several devices (such as a movable bridge) that allow him to tune the banjo differently. When he electrified the instrument, making it sound more like a steel guitar, he drew criticism from many tradition-minded enthusiasts.

Trent signed a recording contract in 1962, and he put out albums periodically through the 1970s. The best-known are his albums with Roy Clark, issued in the mid-1970s. After leaving Wagoner's band, Trent appeared frequently as a member of *Hee Haw* and toured as an opening act for Clark, Dolly Parton, and others. He can be seen regularly at the Buck Trent Dinner Theater in Branson.

The Branson Beat

Shoji Tabuchi's program has become one of Branson's most popular shows despite his lack of hit records or national exposure.

When the Presley family opened the first theater on Highway 76 in Branson in 1967, the traffic was a little easier to navigate. "There just weren't that many people passing through town in those days," the longtime Branson-area performers say.

The Presleys belong to a select group of performers—along with the Mabe brothers, the Plummers, the Braschlers, the Texans, and the Foggy River Boys—who can take credit for creating the family-style entertainment phenomenon in Branson.

Before neon signs flashed the names of internationally known entertainers, these bands were entertaining visitors every day. However, some of them have not been able to survive the flood of more widely recognized performers. Other long-running acts—the Presleys and the Mabes (as the Baldknobbers), for example—continue to draw good-size crowds.

The Branson veteran acts stick with a variety-style formula they've honed for decades. Mainstay Branson performers like the Baldknobbers and Shoji Tabuchi follow a format that has more in common with old-time vaudeville acts or television variety shows than with the slick presentations that mark the concerts of the better-known performers.

"We're very conscious of our heritage," says Gary Presley. "We want to keep the old-time entertainment heritage of the Ozark Mountains alive."

That tradition goes back before the day in 1963 when the Presleys started the Mountain Music Jubilee. Four years later, the Presleys opened a theater on Highway 76. The Presleys consist of Lloyd, his sons Gary and Steve, and their sons Scott,

Greg, Eric, Nick, and John. Gary sings and portrays the dim-witted, athletic humorist Herkimer. Steve acts as band leader and drummer. The third generation of sons plays a variety of instruments and takes turns singing.

The Mabes and their Baldknobbers Hillbilly Jamboree also have several decades of experience entertaining Branson visitors. The family opened its first theater in 1960 in downtown Branson. A Baldknobbers show is a fast-paced variety program that combines the latest country hits with old favorites and splashes of humor.

Shoji Tabuchi, another Branson mainstay, is a Japanese native whose love for traditional American music led him to the Grand Ole Opry and eventually to headlining his own show in the Ozarks. Tabuchi's show, which opened in 1988, features a 13-member cast of singers and dancers, and the program is strong on Broadway-style production numbers.

Bands such as the Baldknobbers (top) and the Presleys (above, showing Herkimer) have entertained in Branson for years, surviving the influx of big name stars through a vaudeville type mix of comedy and music.

The Texans are a youthful quartet of Dallas natives who share the stage with Stars on Revue. The Texans feature lead singer Mark Christian, tenor Paul Acree, baritone Sam Ray, and bass J.D. Kapps. The foursome moved to Branson in 1983. Their show swings through a variety of country, pop, and gospel favorites. The Stars on Revue portion of the show presents from four to six country music veterans, many of them familiar stars from the Grand Ole Opry.

These old-style programs are important to Branson. They give the visitors who travel here an opportunity to enjoy casual, old-fashioned mountain entertainment similar to shows put on in mountain communities in decades past.